CW00863951

# WE
# DON'T
# BLUSH
# ANYMORE

"Were they ashamed when they committed abomination?
No, they were not at all ashamed; they did not know how to BLUSH."
Jeremiah 6:15; 8:12

# WE
# DON'T
# BLUSH
# ANYMORE

The Systematic Destruction of Civility in
## America
*(and what to do about it)*

ROBERT K. PARSONS

XULON PRESS

Xulon Press
2301 Lucien Way #415
Maitland, FL 32751
407.339.4217
www.xulonpress.com

© 2021 by Robert K. Parsons

All rights reserved solely by the author. The author guarantees all
contents are original and do not infringe upon the legal rights of any
other person or work. No part of this book may be reproduced in any
form without the permission of the author. The views expressed in
this book are not necessarily those of the publisher.

Unless otherwise indicated, Scripture quotations taken from the
English Standard Version (ESV). Copyright © 2001 by Crossway, a
publishing ministry of Good News Publishers. Used by permission.
All rights reserved.

Printed in the United States of America.

Paperback ISBN-13: 978-1-6628-1367-2
Dust Jacket ISBN-13: 978-1-6628-1368-9
eBook ISBN-13: 978-1-6628-1369-6

# REVIEWS

Wow. Wow! WE DON'T BLUSH ANYMORE is awesome.
It reads well. It caught and kept my attention.
Robert has much wisdom and recall greatly needed in today's society. He writes from great memory and experience about truths and wisdom that we have lost today. A younger individual could not put it into words or be respected for what is being said.
I learned so much. I was educated. I was enlightened.
Much was brought to my personal senses about how and where we've gone wrong. We let our guard down. We, as Christians, who have the authority and command to keep TRUTH before all mankind, have dropped it to the wayside.
We failed! But we who failed will be made aware of what we need to do.
I was greatly encouraged and challenged. Robert is right on target.

WE DON'T BLUSH ANYMORE is needed!

-David Burton,
davidburtonmnistries.com

*At the beginning of each chapter of this book, you will find these apples of gold. Below each one are fit words, delicious to the soul, "profitable for teaching, for reproof, for correction, and for training in righteousness, that the man of God may be complete, equipped for every good work."*

*2 Timothy 3:16-17*

# PREFACE

As I sit quietly here on my lanai in central Florida looking out over the golf course, all is as peaceful and picturesque as a scene that would grace a picture postcard. Yet, in the pit of my stomach an uneasy feeling is churning and disturbing my serenity. It is my personal opinion that people have become rude, cantankerous, foul-mouthed, foul-thinking, and downright nasty to one another. I am reminded of a description of such people from the Word of God:

> … in the last days there will come times of difficulty. For people will be lovers of self, lovers of money, proud, arrogant, abusive, disobedient to their parents, ungrateful, unholy, heartless, unappeasable, slanderous, without self-control, brutal, not loving good, treacherous, reckless, swollen with conceit, lovers of pleasure rather than lovers of God… (2 Timothy 3:1-4)

I remember better days.

I believe that all of us are responsible and accountable for the decline of civility and decorum in our society and what we do about it.

It used to be that people would blush at a curse word or rude gesture. Now, the use of extremely raunchy vocabulary and behavior is commonplace from young children to older generations.

It ought not to be.

During my career as a chemical engineer, I spent many years in the mountains of North Carolina, and I became personally acquainted with the mountain folks from that area and shall never forget some quaint sayings from a few people. One colloquialism commonly used among them was the phrase, "They don't got no fetchin's up." This phrase became etched in my brain as their apt description of rude, crude, and impolite people. I am fearful that many twenty-first century Americans "don't got no fetchin's up."

To be fair, from Bible times, people have exhibited corrupt minds as Paul detailed in his letters to Timothy. My contention is that America is on a slippery slope to an all-out-degradation, no-holds-barred, type of civilization. We find ourselves sinking into a pit of moral quicksand from which there is no promise of human rescue.

This year, I will celebrate my ninetieth birthday. I look around and see a world in chaos. In years long past I knew a sweeter, gentler era in which people respected one another and had empathy for the feelings of other people. In pondering the state of our nation at this time, I question whether we can ever return to those days of civility.

An old adage states, "If you have to tell others that you are a lady (or gentleman) then you probably aren't." I submit, "If you have to tell others you are a Christian, you probably aren't." Actions will always speak louder than words.

This book is filled with personal observations which presents my view of the past when people were more civil, how we lost the conviction that civility matters, and some suggestions on how we renew our communities, homes, churches, government, and individual lives with God's standard of civility. It will take great effort to reaffirm the solid ground of decency and respect, but the struggle is worth it for those who want to see and live in a more loving and civil society.

We will try to determine who is to blame for this degradation of civility. Can we blame the media? The schools? Our churches? Government? Or do we bring it home to parents?

Can we bring positive and uplifting characteristics back into our personal lives and culture today?

Hopefully, the answers may be found by following the suggestions detailed in this book. "Nothing ventured, nothing gained," is the old saying. Let us venture together.

# DEDICATION

To my sister, Maxine Parsons Cowfer, who went to be with the Lord on December 8, 2020. She was ninety-six years old.

As a little girl of seven years old she took care of me after my mother died. I was only one month old. Maxine was a sweet Christian lady, who cared for others with love and kindness. Even in her later days after multiple medical procedures, she still tried to exemplify civility, love, and thankfulness to her care-givers.

She was my "Little Momma" for a number of years. I knew no other mother. In my young eyes she was ten feet tall. To Maxine, I dedicate this book and write this poem.

<u>Little Momma Ten Foot Tall</u>

My mom was taken away from me
While still a babe and I could not see
Who'd take her place and tend my needs
And soothe my wounds and hear my pleas.

My answer came, He did supply
A sister true to hear my cry
To hold me close lest I should fall
My little momma, ten foot tall.

She wiped my tears and soothed my cries
She held me tight through darkened skies
And never once did she demand
A recompense for her true stand.

Her touch, the kindness of her hand
Gave hope to lift me high to stand
Amidst the world she fashioned me
To be the man that I could be.

A babe had lost a mom so true
But found a love known to a few
And through the years I still rejoice
To know God made the wisest choice.

Today, she's there in Heaven above
And I am left without her love
But the day will come, she'll hear my call
"I'm here, Little Momma, Ten Foot Tall."

# ACKNOWLEDGMENTS

I am deeply indebted to some wonderful elementary school teachers, a Southern gentleman father-in-law, and various men and women throughout my life who epitomized lady-like and gentlemanly conduct.

I honor my daddy who was the sweetest, most humble man I have ever known in my life. He was a man who never said a foul word about another person, yet endured pain and heartache beyond compare. He was a saint.

I acknowledge the help of three special teenagers–Joy and Chloe Wilson, and Will Cotney. They whetted their artistic and writing skills on a difficult subject and excelled in their assignments.

Most of all I am indebted to Maidee, my wonderful wife of sixty-seven years. She is a true lady, who always displays enough Southern charm to fill countless books on civility and good manners. And, she is a whiz at typing and retyping and retyping and... ad infinitum.

While not an active part in the preparation of this book, my son Kenneth (RKP, Jr), is every father's dream. He has demonstrated through all his life gentlemanly characteristics of love, compassion, civility, devotion, and care that makes me proud to be his dad.

Last, but certainly not least, I am blessed with a daughter – Kimberly Parsons Wilson, who meticulously, systematically, and lovingly (she didn't want to hurt Daddy's feelings) brought the words of this book into a coherent readable form. I believe she is really to be acknowledged as the co-author of this book. Thanks, honey.

It is my hope that the conduct and grace of character demonstrated by these special people will return someday to all people here in the greatest country on earth, the United States of America. I pray that we will all be able to blush once again.

RKP

# TABLE OF CONTENTS

Reviews . . . . . . . . . . . . . . . . . . . . . . . . . . . . . . . . . . . . . . . . . . . . . . . . v
Preface . . . . . . . . . . . . . . . . . . . . . . . . . . . . . . . . . . . . . . . . . . . . . . . . ix
Dedication . . . . . . . . . . . . . . . . . . . . . . . . . . . . . . . . . . . . . . . . . . . . . xiii
Acknowledgments . . . . . . . . . . . . . . . . . . . . . . . . . . . . . . . . . . . . . . . xv

**Chapter 1**   The Puritan's Pride . . . . . . . . . . . . . . . . . . . . . . . . . . . 1
**Chapter 2**   McGuffey's Readers. . . . . . . . . . . . . . . . . . . . . . . . . . 12
**Chapter 3**   The Way It Was–Teaching With Foundational
                Truths (A Personal Reflection) . . . . . . . . . . . . . . 22
**Chapter 4**   The Way It Is–Teaching Without
                Foundational Truths. . . . . . . . . . . . . . . . . . . . . . . . 30
**Chapter 5**   The Sad Sixties–Permissiveness Run Amok . . . . . 35
**Chapter 6**   Technology and Social Media . . . . . . . . . . . . . . . . 56
**Chapter 7**   Schools, Society, and Government . . . . . . . . . . . . 67
**Chapter 8**   Protests, Riots, and Anarchy . . . . . . . . . . . . . . . . 85
**Chapter 9**   George Washington's Rules of Civility and
                Decent Behavior . . . . . . . . . . . . . . . . . . . . . . . . . . . 96
**Chapter 10**  Etiquette, Emily Post, and Miss Manners . . . . . . 106
**Chapter 11**  Lagnaippe: Common Sense. . . . . . . . . . . . . . . . . . 112
**Chapter 12**  Family, Faith, and Future . . . . . . . . . . . . . . . . . . . 117
**Chapter 13**  Teen Talk . . . . . . . . . . . . . . . . . . . . . . . . . . . . . . . . 126
**Chapter 14**  Churches and Overseers . . . . . . . . . . . . . . . . . . . 138
**Chapter 15**  Parental Guidance and Involvement . . . . . . . . . 159
**Chapter 16**  Turning It Around . . . . . . . . . . . . . . . . . . . . . . . . 178

Final Thoughts . . . . . . . . . . . . . . . . . . . . . . . . . . . . . . . . . . . . . . . . . 189
Biography. . . . . . . . . . . . . . . . . . . . . . . . . . . . . . . . . . . . . . . . . . . . . . 191
Bibliography . . . . . . . . . . . . . . . . . . . . . . . . . . . . . . . . . . . . . . . . . . . 193

# Chapter One

# THE PURITAN'S PRIDE

*"Do not be deceived: 'Bad company ruins good morals.'"*
I Corinthians 15:33

T he foundation of beginning education for our forefathers as
they landed and took up abode in this new nation was, first
and foremost, *The New England Primer*. It was compiled and published around 1688 by Benjamin Harris, a British journalist who
emigrated to Boston. Harris' textbook, the first printed in America,
was *the* textbook for the masses. This textbook, alongside the Holy
Bible, gave all the instructions necessary for living a pleasing and
civil life. The colonists' standard of deportment and conduct was
based on the principles found and exercised in the *Primer*. Harris
promoted literacy through his short book, but he also revealed
aspects of the English Puritan culture, which found fertile ground
in the lives of early Americans ("The New-England Primer"). The
textbook was used well into the twentieth century in its nearly
original version.

A look at the *Primer* would set the American Civil Liberties
Union on the warpath today since it includes as its primary
teaching tool the Word of God. From beginning to end, there are
biblical references interspersed with English grammar lessons. I

am struck by the Puritan's deliberate plan to educate their children with a solid biblical doctrine, emphasizing spiritual as well as intellectual mastery.

As can be seen below in the *Primer's* alphabet lessons, each letter is emphasized and then connected to a Bible verse that brings with it a message of moral conduct and living. If our public schools of today used this *New England Primer,* we might be able to bring a transformation to our nation that would restore patriotism, morality, individual self-esteem and overall civility. Our forefathers knew what they were teaching, and they made one of the most moral nations history has ever known. How sad that we rejected and abandoned our national model and stumbled far down the road of degradation and incivility.

*************************

## An Alphabet of Lessons for Youth

**A** wise son maketh a glad father, but a foolish son is the heaviness of his mother. (Proverbs 10:1)

**B**etter is a little with the fear of the Lord, than great treasure & trouble therewith. (Proverbs 15:16)

**C**ome unto Christ all ye that labor and are heavy laden and he will give you rest. (Matthew 11:28)

**D**o not the abominable thing which I hate saith the Lord. (Jeremiah 44:4b)

**E**xcept a man be born again, he cannot see the kingdom of God. (John 3:3b)

Foolishness is bound up in the heart of a child, but the rod of correction shall drive it far from him. (Proverbs 22:15)

Godliness is profitable unto all things, having the promise of the life that now is and that which is to come. (1 Timothy 4:8)

Holiness becomes GOD's house forever. (Psalm 93:5b)

It is good for me to draw near unto GOD. (Psalm 73:28)

Keep thy heart with all diligence, for out of it are the issues of life. (Proverbs 4:23)

Liars shall have their part in the lake which burns with fire and brimstone. (Revelation 21:8)

Many are the afflictions of the righteous, but the LORD delivereth them out of them all. (Psalm 34:19)

Now is the accepted time, now is the day of salvation. (2 Corinthians 6:2b)

Out of the abundance of the heart the mouth speaketh. (Matthew 12:34b)

Pray to thy Father which is in secret; and thy Father which sees in secret shall reward thee openly. (Matthew 6:6b)

Quit you like men, be strong, stand fast in the faith. (1 Cor. 16:13b)

Remember thy Creator in the days of thy youth. (Ecclesiastes 12:1)

Seest thou a man wise in his own conceit, there is more hope of a fool than of him. (Proverbs 26:12)

Trust in GOD at all times, ye people, pour out your hearts before him. (Psalm 61:8)

Upon the wicked, God shall rain an horrible tempest. (Psalm 11:6)

Wo to the wicked, it shall be ill with him, for the reward of his hands shall be given him. (Isaiah 3:11)

eXhort one another daily while it is called to day, lest any of you be hardened thro' the deceitfulness of sin. (Hebrews 3:13)

Young men ye have overcome the wicked one. (1 John 2:14)

Zeal hath consumed me, because thy enemies have forgotten the word of God. (Psalm 119:139)

Notes:

- In the *Primer*, only the Bible verses are provided for each letter. I have included references in parentheses for your further study. In order to fit the acrostic pattern, the author re-worded verses from the King James Version.
- David Barton explains in his "Helpful Notes to the Reader" that the original text used "f" and "ff" (or *f* and *ff*) for "s" and "ss." In this chapter, I used "s" and "ss" for ease of reading,

but it would be a good challenge for you to try to decode the original.

- You will notice that the letters *J* and *V* are missing. Early on, in various written documents, *i* and *j* were used interchangeably, as were *u* and *v*. If I could make an addition to this precious text for those two letters, I would suggest any one of the choices provided below:

Jesus called a little child unto Him. (Matthew 18:2) OR
Jesus knew their thoughts. (Matthew 12:25) OR
Jesus wept. (John 11:35)

- -

Vengeance is mine, I will repay, sayeth the Lord. (Romans 12:19)
Violence covers the mouth of the wicked, but blessings are on the head of the just. (Proverbs 12:6)

While many other Scriptures could be used for the j letter study, the provided ones give the young child an insight into the characteristics of Jesus that are easily understood. Jesus loves little children. He knows the thoughts of all people. He demonstrated genuine grief over the death of His friend, Lazarus (John 11:35) and the impending destruction of Jerusalem (Luke 19:41). These verses teach children that Jesus is God, but He is also human. As children relate to Jesus' human emotion of weeping, they receive a powerful connection to Him, in addition to the practical grammar and scriptural messages from the text.

As colonial children progressed through the letters of the alphabet in the *Primer*, Bible truths were abundant. Keep in mind, the child memorized each letter with its related Bible verse; this was of the utmost importance in memorization and retention. Scholars agree that association is a great tool for recalling specific details. Our forefathers, in their simple method of teaching, knew this type of education would work. It did work for centuries, until our modern educators presented a new educational system that started dumbing down our children and youth into non-thinking and non-productive miscreants.

If we were still teaching these attributes in our modern classrooms, our society would be so much better and civil. Would we see less violence in our schools, on our playgrounds, and on our streets? I believe so. Mass violence and disrespect was uncommon in the communities of those who grew up on *Primer* teachings. When there was some rebellious youngster in school, discipline was exercised with the intentional purpose of turning the student back toward a right attitude and behavior.

## Children's Prayers

A familiar prayer made an appearance in *The New England Primer* and it still stands today as a common bedtime prayer. It reads:

Now I lay me down to sleep,
I pray the Lord my soul to keep,
If I should die before I wake,
I pray the Lord my soul to take (sec. 2).

From this poem, and others that are included in the *Primer*, comes an appreciation of poetic rhythm as well as truths of biblical principles such as honesty, duty, the golden rule, and love and trust in God. Disobedience to any of these principles brought shame and embarrassment on the individual, their family, and community. That shame would undoubtedly have brought a blush to the cheeks of the transgressor. How sad that these principles are not taught today in our schools. It would be a far, far sweeter world if they were.

## Catechism and Spiritual Milk for American Babes

The teaching of catechism (doctrines) and spiritual milk (basic instructions) as presented in the *Primer* is so astoundingly biblical that it sets one to thinking that our forefathers gave no thought to the separation of church and state. As a matter of fact, they insisted that biblical principles be taught in every school, and to every child. How is this for an early "no child left behind" policy? Every child understood and accepted that these teachings were for their betterment, in order for them to succeed in life and maintain a moral and just person and society. Our nation prospered and grew into the envy of the world based upon our foundations of freedom, justice, and civility.

One hundred seven questions and answers found in the *Primer* catechism teach such doctrine as the chief end of man, creation, sin, redemption, moral law, faith, church sacraments, and prayer (secs. 2*–3*).

John Cotton drew up an additional list of questions and answers to nourish the soul and provide a comprehensive, uniform standard of beliefs (sec. 3*).

Some may question the method of making everyone believe and recite the same religious dogma. What if people had different beliefs about God or no belief at all? What if parents didn't want their children indoctrinated by biblical teaching? At this time, parents were not mandated to send their children to school. It must be understood that the whole purpose of the New England colonies was freedom of religion and the furtherance of the Gospel. The colonists were in agreement on matters of faith. With the wide spread consensus of a biblical foundation, entire communities and colonies upheld the same standard of living.

Written into the 1629 *Massachusetts Bay Charter* is the declaration that the people may be so religiously, peaceably, and civilly governed that their good life and orderly conversations may win others to the knowledge and obedience of the only true God and Savior of man and the Christian faith, which was their full intention and principal end of the colony ("The Massachusetts Bay Charter").

## A Dialogue between Christ, Youth, and the Devil

*The New England Primer* ends with a dialogue detailing the temptation of a youth falling prey to Satan. It is a battle of life and shows the efforts of Christ to persuade the youth to follow Him on the straight and narrow way leading to eternity, versus traversing the broad road leading to eternal separation from God. All of the dialogue was written in verse, of which a portion has been printed here:

YOUTH:
> Those days which God to me doth send,
> In pleasure I'm resolv'd to spend;
> Though parents grieve and me correct,
> Yet I their counsel will reject.

DEVIL:
> The resolution which you take,
> Sweet youth it doth me merry make.
> And learn to lie, and curse and swear,
> And be as proud as any are;
> Yea, fight and scratch, and also bite,
> Then in thee I will take delight.

YOUTH:
> My heart against my parents now,

Shall harden'd be, and will not bow:
I won't submit at all to them,
But all good counsels will condemn,

CHRIST:
Wilt thou, O youth make such a choice,
And thus obey the devil's voice!
The Devil and his ways defy,
Believe him not, he doth but lie:
His ways seem sweet, but youth beware,
He for thy soul hath laid a snare.

YOUTH:
Moreover, this I also know,
Thou can'st at last great mercy show.
When I am old, and pleasure gone,
Then what thou say'st I'll think upon.

CHRIST:
Nay, hold vain youth, thy time is short,
I have thy breath, I'll end thy sport;

THE CONCLUSION:
Thus end the days of woful youth,
Who won't obey nor mind the truth;
Nor hearken to what preachers say,
But do their parents disobey.
They in their youth go down to hell,
Under eternal wrath to dwell.
Many don't live out half their days,
For cleaving unto sinful ways (secs. 4-4*).

While this excerpt from the "Dialogue" shows only a portion of the imagined conversation, it speaks to the heart of the youth at that time. If only our youth in the twenty-first century would listen and heed these wise words, they would grasp truths that are everlasting and edifying. It seems that many are not listening and our society is in a free-fall away from civility.

Even though *The New England Primer* was used as the main reading textbook for the new colonies into the twentieth century, Noah Webster's *American Spelling Book* (also known as the *Blue Back Speller*) became another go-to text around 1783. It was part of the three-volume collection *A Grammatical Institute of the English Language* which included a speller, a grammar, and a reader book. These key textbooks of the early Americans were used for the next hundred years, only to be supplanted by *McGuffey's Readers*. Most of the *Speller* lessons gave instructions on correct pronunciation of letters, syllables, short and long words, compound words, American state names, topographical labels, and much more. The *Speller* contained biblical instructions cloaked in everyday jargon and stories. Many of the sayings, quotes, and themes can be closely linked to proverbs found in the Old Testament of the Bible.

In the final pages of Webster's *Speller*, he presents "A Moral Catechism." He begins by asking about moral virtue and what rules "direct us in our moral conduct." His clear answer is that all the necessary rules for good conduct are to be found in God's Word, the Bible. Webster continues his moral catechism on such topics as Humility, Purity of Heart, and Gratitude (secs. N2-0).

Here is a portion of a lesson on civility from "The Sisters":

> Does the heart want culture? Weed out the noxious passions from the heart, as you would hurtful plants from among the flowers. Cherish the virtues–love, kindness, meekness, modesty, goodness. Let

them thrive, and produce their natural fruit, pure
happiness, and joys serene through life (sec. G).

The spiritual impact of *The New England Primer* and the *Blue Back Speller* on the moral character of the people of the New World cannot be minimized. The Bible was the heart and soul of the mechanisms that influenced all of Puritan life. Our founding fathers were obedient to its call and direction, and they included its teachings in almost every document written during those early days. This nation thrived by honoring God and His Word as a compass for morality, ethical behavior, and individual compassion for neighbors. Any breach of the moral directives contained in the Bible and the textbooks was an embarrassment and resulted in the hanging of the head in shame.

And maybe, just maybe, a blush or two might have appeared on their cheeks.

# Chapter Two

# MCGUFFEY'S READERS

*"For he that would love life and see good days ...*
*let him eschew evil and do good."*

1 Peter 3:10-11 KJV

S ince 1836, millions of boys and girls have acquired a solid education from the classic *McGuffey's Readers*. Where the Puritan's *New England Primer* and the *Blue Back Speller* left off, the *Readers* picked up and embellished the rudiments of education. John H. Westerhoff explains that William H. McGuffey was one of the most influential figures in the history of public education. He was known as *"the* schoolmaster of the nation!"* (13). Westerhoff hits to the heart of this chapter as he mentions a 1927 newspaper article claiming that "with the exception of the Bible, McGuffey's Readers represent the most significant force in the framing of our national morals and tastes" (qtd. in Westerhoff 15).

As a strong proponent of public education, McGuffey sought to fashion a curriculum of moral and spiritual education for nine-teenth-century American students. Over the years, two more editions of the *Readers* were published, but most of the religious tenets were eliminated from the texts. Moral lessons remained, adjusted and updated for an American civil religion that appealed to middle-class, rural citizens. Westerhoff states that McGuffey would probably not have been happy with the changes. Even though the focus of the *Reader's* lessons shifted from theology and ethics, there still remained the moral, cultural, and intellectual values important to families and communities. (18-19)

It is interesting to note that McGuffey created a public school curriculum that withstood the publishing changes deemed necessary for a changing world. Though the Christian worldview of 1836 was eventually removed from the public education curriculum, we still had educational materials crucial for understanding civility, etiquette, good manners, and character. (20)

The *McGuffey Readers* are in a group referred to as *eclectic* – composed of material gathered from various sources and systems ("Eclectic"). McGuffey pulled the content for the *Eclectic* version together from existing textbooks to meet a basic need of a growing nation (21). There needed to be quality education conveyed which instructed children in patriotism, civic response, cultural assimilation, and occupational training. Interspersed throughout the lessons, the biblical principles spoke to the moral character of the student as well as the intellectual character. Teachers were expected to mold young minds of America in piety, character, and community values. (22)

Future American leaders were taught in the one-room schoolhouses of yesteryear, or by the fireplace of the homeschooling family. Even today, some homeschoolers are still using the *Readers* for part of their curriculum, much to the consternation of the public school gurus who have watered down the government-mandated curriculum. We often see that the grades and deportment of parochial and homeschooled students far exceed many of those in public schools. Likewise, perhaps the basic principles of the *Readers* far exceed all the new ideologies in our public school system curricula today.

The stories from the *Readers* are timeless and priceless, such as the simple story of how to determine cardinal directions when in nature. Outside, the reader is to observe the direction of the sunrise and extend the left arm in that direction. In front of the person is south, behind is north, and on the right is west. What a simple, yet practical way to determine directions, while possibly saving a lad or lass from being lost in the forests of that time (*Second Reader*, Lesson XXXIV, "The Points of the Compass," 79-81). This, however, is only the beginning of the depth of teaching put forth in *McGuffey's Readers*.

Themes of honest work, kindness, forgiveness, moral direction, and integrity leap from the pages of the *Primer* all the way to the *Fourth Reader* to instruct the student and build character. The intertwining of biblical principles and common-sense living are foundations which students and adults must have to live a happy and productive life. These principles also provide the tools to maintain a life of civility and be a blessing to others. Reading texts in today's schools address some issues such as honesty, compassion, and inclusion, but not from a biblical perspective. Without the standard of the Bible, there can be no clear and accurate understanding of right from wrong. The separation of church and state prohibit this biblical teaching to the detriment of the student.

What have the teachings in the *Readers* to do with blushing, you may ask?

Blushing is not always demonstrated by rose-colored cheeks. Blushing can refer to the embarrassment of an individual which impinges negatively on his character and moral standing. The *Readers* teach many stories that focus on character. They help build a concrete foundation of positive morals for the student to carry with him all his life. Properly taught and learned, these principles will stay with the student into adulthood. Any assault on these principles should result in embarrassing or blushing episodes.

Provided below are examples from the four original *Readers*, highlighting some key moral lessons.

*McGuffey's Eclectic First Reader* focuses on reading and spelling. As students work through the lessons the stories advance topics such as nature, children and animals, kindness, goodness, racial equality, prayer, and honesty.

## Benevolence (First Reader, Lesson IX, (The Poor Old Man)

This story-lesson teaches the attribute of kindness to the poor. The author writes of a beggar visiting a home to ask for food, where he is given food, clothes, and shoes. Jane, the model character for the student-reader, is instructed not to give the beggar money to buy shoes, but to actually give him shoes. How insightful this is to provide a specific need, recognizing that we should do for others what we would want them to do for us. In doing so the student is instructed to look to God for all things. This is a lesson in love with direction.

Many poor and homeless people are seen begging along the roads and highways in cities today. Some are truly in need and they should be helped, but sometimes it is difficult to know the status of everyone we see. Benevolence can best be equitably distributed through the church. Read the references to the early church in the book of Acts. In these passages, believers contributed to the needs of others so that they "had all things in common," (Acts 2:42-47) and were "distributing proceeds to each as any had need" (Acts 4:32-37). Giving to those on the side of the road lies in the heart of the donor. Jesus tells His followers that "It is more blessed to give than receive" (Acts 20:35).

It is apparent that the intention of the stories in McGuffey's was to lead students to model their lives after biblical principles.

Kindness, compassion, and generosity are all part of this lesson on benevolence. (15-18)

The *Eclectic Second Reader* also focuses on reading and spelling. Eighty-five stories are provided dealing with idleness, sibling love, greed, nature and animals, diligence, King Solomon, God, Creation, honesty, disobedience, the Ten Commandments, and profane language.

## Integrity and Courage (Second Reader, Lesson LVII, True Courage)

In this story about true integrity, James and Henry are tempting George to throw a snowball at the schoolhouse front door. What a typical scene from childhood this is; I remember one similar in my life. George resists their taunts but is branded a coward and severely harassed for his stance. Finally, George weakens and throws the snowball, only to be caught and punished.

This story guides students to realize that there will be occasions when it will require a severe struggle to preserve personal integrity. It takes courage to stand strong and not give in to something that is morally wrong. Each person must act right, unmoved by the threats or flattery of others.

James and Henry are bullies. To stand alone in the face of ridicule and mockery is a common situation in our society. It takes true courage to be strong and unafraid of what others may do to you or your loved ones. (145-149)

## Honesty (Second Reader, Lesson LXI, The Little Boy and the Hatchet)

Honesty is the quintessential foundation of George Washington's character. Washington's goodness and honesty of character were taught to every student in the nation. George was a person to admire and emulate. This old story does not get the recognition that it deserves among schoolchildren of today.

Young Washington's father taught his son about truth, purity, and dependability. He exclaimed that he would ride fifty miles to see a boy of this quality. At the same time, George's father stated that he was willing to put his son in a coffin and place him in a grave rather than see him to be a liar.

What an interesting point is made in this relationship of father to son. Father Washington was insistent on teaching his son about civility and honesty, and he took the time to invest in his son's life and character. George even wrote a book of rules for civility. We'll look at that later in this book. George carried his father's effective training over into his adult life and his dealings with soldiers, national leaders, and common people.

In the *Reader's* story, six-year-old George is given a hatchet with which he went about chopping everything in his way. What little boy, who has grown up outside the city lights, hasn't experienced something like this? A hatchet, a saw, a hammer or a toy gun—all become playthings in the hands of a little boy.

George faces the dilemma of confessing his destruction of his father's favorite cherry tree. He could not lie. Father Washington was so happy with George's honesty; he considered his son's truthfulness to be of more value than thousands of gold trees.

This story became etched in the minds of children who were encouraged to face the consequences of a mischievous deed with integrity and honesty. That was the moral lesson taught to yesterday's students. It resonated off the walls of schoolhouses and produced a people with sound character and moral attributes capable of building a strong, reliable, and decent nation. (158-162)

The *Eclectic Third Reader* shifts from grammatical concepts to literature of the best American and English writers. Prose and poetry are introduced, with plain rules for reading. In this book, we see stories about the Bible, Jesus Christ, the rainbow, the Sermon on the Mount, the goodness of God, the Gospel, and the nineteenth Psalm. All are nestled among more nature and animal themes.

## Virtue (Third Reader, Lesson XVIII, The Bible)

"Rule–Read for improvement, and not for show. The great object of reading is to improve your minds in useful knowledge, to establish your hearts in virtue, and to prepare you for a right performance of the duties of life" (67).

Permit the gist of the above Rule to be absorbed into your minds thoroughly. Schoolchildren were admonished to read for improvement, virtue, and rightness of mind and not to show off. In doing these tasks, they were prepared to act right in life. They became gentlemen and ladies by deed and not by word only.

This is a simple lesson about the Bible. The excellency of the Bible is instilled in the hearts and minds of students. A history of the antiquity of the Bible is given to undergird the Holiness of the Bible and its inspired contents. The Scriptures were supernaturally influenced by the Holy Spirit in the lives of ancient prophets to direct them to write down God's absolute thoughts and directions to man, in order for him to rule over animals and beasts of the field and attain the glory of Heaven through the only begotten Son of God. (67-73)

The *Eclectic Fourth Reader,* more advanced than the *Third Reader,* is a smorgasbord of prose and poetry from American and English writers, but it adds copious rules for reading. Oh, that modern-day readers could attain to the loftiness of these stories would be a dream come true. The student is carried through the lessons with words of encouragement, wisdom, and edification that permit him or her to desire excellence in mastery of the content. Time is of the essence. Hasten reader and read, before these stories slip away into obscurity.

## (Fourth Reader, Suggestions to Teachers)

To read aloud or not to read aloud, that is the question.

Throughout the teachings of the *Readers*, the importance of reading is emphasized. It was of critical importance to teach students that reading was to be out loud and standing in front of peers. Today, many students, and even adults, lack the essentials of public reading skills. The embarrassment and blushing that takes place when asked to read aloud is beyond the pale. The beauty of the *Readers* is magnified by the instructions to read aloud. This directive is paramount and to be followed to the letter. Students of the *Readers* are to stand tall and proud throughout their lives. Tone, enunciation, inflection, clarity, and emphasis are reading skills that good readers master.

## (Fourth Reader, Lesson XV, On Elocution and Reading)

The business of training our youth in elocution must be commenced in childhood. The first school is the nursery. There, at least, may be formed a distinct articulation, which is the first requisite for good speaking. How rarely is it found in perfection among our orators! Words, says one, referring to articulation, should 'be delivered out from the lips, as beautiful coins, newly issued from the mint, deeply and accurately impressed, perfectly finished, neatly struck by the proper organs, distinct, in due succession, and of due weight.' ... Grace in eloquence – in the pulpit, at the bar – cannot be separated from grace in the ordinary manners, in private life, in the social circle, in the family. ... You may, therefore, begin the work of forming the orator with your child, not merely by teaching him to declaim, but what is of more consequence, by observing and correcting his daily manners, motions, and attitudes. (56-57)

It should be essential in our classrooms that the same pains and discipline devoted to forming an accomplished performer on a musical instrument be devoted to acquiring good reading skills. Let there be masters of the reading voice who produce a symphony of sound resonating from the lips, and let the inner being burst forth from young and old, to drown out the cacophony of crude, rude, and undisciplined discord. We need these orators today.

Reviewing the whole of the *Fourth Reader* is beyond the scope of this chapter. However, please review the following selection of chapter titles with short synopses and savor the rich beauty and broad themes that were used to lift the characters of our forefathers and mothers.

## Lessons XVI and Lesson XVII–Necessity of Education

These two lessons give the plea to educate the people of this great land. Patriots of the four corners of the country are reminded that we, the United States of America, are "useless without the supervening influence of the government of God." There must be "education of the head and heart of the nation" (59-64).

## Lesson XXIII–Character of Wilberforce

This description of the character of William Wilberforce stems primarily from his eloquent speeches given to the British Parliament. The diction, tone, and inspirational qualities of his speech held listeners spellbound, even in his simplest of presentations. The man who helped abolish the slave trade in England was highly admired for his oratorical abilities (81-82).

## Lesson XXXII – Elevated Character of Woman

In this age when women are championing equality, claiming that there has never been respect for the female gender, this lesson elevates the character of women as neighbors, friends, daughters, wives and mothers. Never let it be said that men have historically devalued women. In fact, the author seems to place women on a pedestal as they demonstrate kindness to the sick, respect for the elderly, devotion to children, loyalty to husband, and strength through her relationship with Christ. As a woman demonstrates moral character and civility to all, generations of children see a blessed example lived out in front of them (104-106).

• Lessons LIV, LV, and LXIII are a select few that expound the basic teachings of God's Word. Throughout the entire *Reader* series, all character building, learning, accomplishments, and morality have been based on the absolute study and application of biblical precepts. To promote anything less would weaken our society and possibly move us toward a totalitarian government. Studying and following God's Word builds character, morality, and good citizens. These are the overall themes throughout the *Readers*.

This tantalizing review of the *McGuffey's Readers* clearly shows the depth and breadth of the subjects. When studied carefully, they can lead to the development of educated, considerate, moral and civil citizens of a nation. These teachings should be reinstituted in the public-school curriculum today so that we may begin producing children who will be a blessing to their parents, peers, and posterity.

Chapter Three

# THE WAY IT WAS– TEACHING WITH FOUNDATIONAL TRUTHS (A PERSONAL REFLECTION)

*"Train up a child in the way he should go; even when he is old he will not depart from it."*

Proverbs 22:6

The time was 1936. The place was Roosevelt Grade School in East Akron, Ohio.

The class size in Mrs. Wolfe's first grade class was 48. I was there with 47 other urchins, hip-deep in the Depression, ready to play softball and enjoy recess.

Phooey on learning! At least that's what I thought. My reading was very poor, close to non-existent.

My mother had died from a burst appendix when I was one month old, and my preschool training consisted of a few instructions from my older sister who acted as my surrogate mom.

Dad was still reconstructing his life to try and take care of four young'uns, of which I was the youngest. It really was one of those "times that try men's souls" (Paine). There was so much poverty everywhere. We all needed help just to stay alive and make ends meet. In this environment I began my education.

The reliance on my elementary teachers, Mrs. Flatten, Mrs. Libis, Mrs. Paine (and she was), and Principal Fraley, for detailed instructions in all matters was accepted without question. We read the Bible every morning, along with reciting the Pledge of Allegiance. Each day at lunch we uttered: "Heavenly Father, hear us say, thank You for this food today. Amen."

Never a day went by that we did not pray in this way. No one questioned it.

As time and my learning progressed over the next ten years, a phenomenal transition took place in my character and moral make-up. My tone of civility and good manners was not polished, but the rough edges were being smoothed and refined. Common reminders came repeatedly:

"Remove your hat when entering a building."
"Do not chew gum in the school."
"Say 'thank you.'"
"Comb your hair."
"Wipe your feet before entering the schoolhouse."
"Ladies before gentlemen."
"Bring and use your hankie."
"No talking or shoving in line."
"Wash your hands after going to the bathroom."

Wow! So many rules! How could I ever remember all of them?

If any one of us was called out in front of the class for a transgression of these laws of the schoolhouse, it was a matter of total embarrassment and blushing. Each teacher had her or his special list of rules to follow. Any deviation from that list was a severe breach of etiquette and good manners. Punishment for infractions was swift and sure.

Under those conditions, strange things happened to me and my classmates. Most of us came away from those formative years with better character, stronger moral standards, appreciation for authority, obedience to edifying laws, and yes, good conduct. We were better humans and citizens of this nation because teachers cared for us and our character. They invested in training our bodies, minds, souls, and spirits. We were guided into a loftier standard than the shallow teachings of today.

Teaching a large classroom of Depression-era waifs was a monumental task. My friends and I were more interested in what we were having for lunch even though most of us knew there was just a plain bologna sandwich double-wrapped in wax paper and yesterday's newspaper. The bologna was purchased on credit at the local jot-em-down store, to be paid for as soon as Dad could afford it. Those who brought lunch in a metal pail were the "ritzies," with delectable morsels to savor.

Our schoolroom was a pleasant place. It was peaceful, joyful, and safe. Even though many children in America lost their innocent childhoods due to deprivation and want during that time, when we entered the school building, we entered a sanctuary from the cares of the Depression. Even while we all struggled to survive, we were educated into strong and civil citizens.

Learning was based on rising above the place we existed every day and pursuing the American dream of the good life. Families had no handouts, no welfare, no food stamps, no hospitalization, and no workmen's compensation. We just had the guts to keep learning as we did our best to take a step or two up.

I remember that my teachers were ogres of the first kind, but we all loved them anyway. We learned by rote memorization. We stated our math, history, or grammar facts over and over until they created a deep rut in our brains. We stood, we recited, and we did our multiplication tables through a challenge game using display cards. It was fun, and we all tried to beat Mary, the teacher's pet. We did improve, without harboring any feeling of inferiority or low self-esteem when we didn't get an award just for participation.

The government did intervene superficially in those days. We received free grapefruit juice at lunch to keep the rickets away. I can still taste that sour juice. And once a year we were visited by a mobile dental clinic. How I hated those dental clinic doctors who performed many procedures with minimal Novocain. Ouch!!!

Three important things happened to me in elementary school.

1) I grew from a snotty-nosed, uncouth Depression kid to a young man with personal habits just a little above a Banshee. I was making progress, and by the time I was out of elementary school, my shoes were shined, and my hair was combed daily. I had a hanky, and I used it properly. My hat was removed, my gum was out, and I treated others with respect because that's what people with good manners did. I learned all that before I turned twelve. Was I ever making progress!

2) I had a feeling of unity with my schoolmates that I miss to this very day. We were all together in this thing called life. We experienced growing up in hard times, and we made it. We had little, but cared for little, other than some food, a pair of shoes, some overalls to wear, and a place to call home with mom and dad. We were trying to read, write, and do our numbers. Not all of us succeeded, and some were even kept back for a year. They needed more practice in those rote lessons that were

pounded into our brains at a relentless and systematic pace. Most of my fellow classmates did succeed. They went to high school and beyond, to perfect those new-found character gems we learned early in life.

3) I discovered girls! Now, a whole new strange set of manners needed to be ingrained into my brain in order for me to appear civil and couth to the opposite sex. The teachers were not much help with this except to insist on politeness and kindness when dealing with young ladies. The grooves of politeness are still deep in my brain, and politeness reigns supreme when interacting with yon fair young maidens.

## ONE THING MORE

4) I was sustained by the practice of Bible reading, prayer, and patriotism. I grew up in a home where my daddy insisted on the daily discipline of spiritual growth and relationship with God. Home values, and the school support of these same values, set a standard that remains in my life to this day. All students participated in our morning Bible reading and prayer, and no one was offended. At that time, there was no revolt from the American Civil Liberties Union, Atheist Union, or other anti-God organizations. There were just boys and girls seeking a better life, and teachers who believed that the way to the better life included patterning one's life after the principles espoused in God's Holy Word.

I think, for the most part, it worked pretty well for most all of us.

All was not perfect in the old days. We had bullies then, too. However, there was a system to deal with them. The first line of defense was the homeroom teacher with various means of correction for those sweet darlings. Punishment included writing "I will not bully" 100 times on the blackboard, followed by a week of washing that blackboard. Most often, the bully was blushing and highly embarrassed by standing in front of the class while writing on the blackboard. Sometimes there were a few whacks across the open palm with a ruler. Every punishment was preceded by a warning-sometimes many. The wayfaring urchin was warned once again to stop bullying and mind his manners.

But there was more. If the bullying continued, the offender was escorted to the principal's office for a consultation. Several steps were followed for the purpose of correction, never abuse.

1) In the first meeting, the bully was warned of the error, and his or her name was written into the principal's little black book.

2) In the second meeting, the bully's parents were called and informed of the problem. They were requested to correct the problem at home. They were then reminded that if another issue took place, the board of education would be applied to the seat of understanding. Ouch! His name was written a second time in the principal's black book; beware a third time.

3) In the third meeting, the hammer was dropped. The principal applied the board of education to the offender's buttocks in five well-placed whacks. In case some of you do not know what a board of education is, it is a paddle approximately 3 inches wide by 18 inches long by 1 inch thick. This was applied carefully and lovingly to "the setter down place" as my daddy called it.

Not many students went this far. Those who did seemed to improve their manners and resist bullying. Their ego was bruised, and their eyes watered, but their life was not destroyed. As a matter of fact, their lives usually changed for the better. This punishment, with lots of love, did work. It would still work today if we were brave enough to try it.

My memories of a better era involve the civil, moral, intellectual, educational, and spiritual truths instilled by caring parents working in conjunction with teachers and the church to produce strong and faithful future citizens of this nation.

In my time, teachers had some leeway in what and how they taught. Biblical lessons, similar to those in the *McGuffey Readers,* were still presented.

That was then, and times have changed to more humane disciplinary treatments of erring waifs within the school systems of today. Before we advance into what was lost, let's define foundational truths that should be established in the lives of decent, God-fearing people.

For the definition of foundational truths as we discuss in this book, *Webster's Dictionary* gives the following information:

> foundation–a base upon which something rests, stands, or is supported.
> truths–conformity and/or total agreement with reality or undisputable facts.

Therefore, foundational truths are those truths which form the platform upon which a person's life is established and built. It must be understood that some people have foundational truths and some do not.

For the purposes of this book, the beliefs that establish a person's wholesome character and life come directly from Judeo-Christian teachings. Our faith is built on Jesus Christ and His Word. Our foundation is built on the solid rock that will withstand the adversities of life.

# Chapter Four

# THE WAY IT IS– TEACHING WITHOUT FOUNDATIONAL TRUTHS

*"Woe to those who call evil good and good evil, who put darkness for light and light for darkness, who put bitter for sweet and sweet for bitter!"*

Isaiah 5:20

When did we lose our foundational truths based on a solid biblical foundation? I saw them receding as I moved through elementary school into high school in the late 1940s. While we balanced on some semblances of standard morality, our biblical and civil platform was beginning to break apart.

We have already defined foundational truths in the previous chapter. A more general application of foundational truths could be: beliefs that establish basic standards of civility and decorum of a person's character and life. When the sickening Sixties arrived, the teaching of foundational truths and biblical based character was well on the way out of the classroom by government decree.

The systematic destruction of civility began in earnest in the early 1960s. Murder became a woman's choice when abortion was legalized. Prayer and Bible reading were deemed unlawful in public schools. The descent into darkness began when we released our grip on civil and moral standards, and very few were trying to put on the brakes.

In order for a society to maintain its social stability, there must be a belief in something greater than self. The Bible tells us that man is sinful from the time of conception. Children do not have to be taught how to sin. They do it automatically; it is their nature. We are born in sin. Therefore, we each must be taught truths that help us to overcome the inherent nature of birth. We must be introduced to beliefs that help us rise above the beasts of the field. But where do we find these truths? Where do we find building blocks for a foundation that will withstand the storms of life?

Down through the centuries great philosophers and scholars put forth their agendas for the good life. Some of these ideas were good, but many were lacking in sustainability. They worked for a short time, but eventually petered out when the pressures of society (modernization) overpowered them.

In the beginning, God created a standard of behavior. He gave Adam and Eve freedom with limits. Later, He provided laws to establish and maintain civil obedience and peace in order that man could live in relationship to God and with humans. We see these laws disregarded today. They are not taught in our public schools, few places of worship, or many homes.

Once upon a time, and I use the phrase "once upon a time" because I feel like I may have been part of a fairy tale–a time when we were taught foundational truths and laws. Our forefathers knew these truths were essential to the basic societal structure of humanity. Consequently, they put into place schools, teachers, and curriculum that would teach the truth that would keep men free and civil throughout the tides of time. Refer to the previous chapters where I discussed the early curriculum of colonial schools.

Specific truths were taught and drilled into the minds and psyche of colonial and early American children. These truths were absorbed and lived out in daily life. Today, we see reduced standards of civility in our communities, and people who hold these truths dear are slowly fading from influencing society.

So, what are these truths and laws? Our founding fathers relied on the Holy Bible for their standard. They used the Ten Commandments, the teachings of Jesus, and the teachings of the Apostles to lay the foundation upon which all men and societies should build a civil and respectful society.

In the previous chapter, I described the process for disciplining wayward students during my early school years. Foundational truths are now being replaced with relative morality.

Today, Johnny is supported by liberated parents who oppose corrective discipline in any form. In addition, Johnny's rights are protected by numerous organizations such as the ACLU, the Teacher's Union, or the school boards. Consequently, little Johnny must not be embarrassed in any way because this will bring emotional trauma and stifle his progressive spirit. So, the sweet young thing is sent for counseling where he is left to play his favorite video game. He is not punished nor confronted with his crime against a classmate. He is not inclined to feel sorry for his deed. He is not embarrassed and does not blush.

If the problems with Johnny continue, parents may be informed that their little angel is subject to discipline or expulsion from school. Therein, the path is opened wide for Johnny's parents or concerned organizations to begin litigation against the school, the principal, the teacher, or even the child's victim and his or her parents. After all, Johnny has rights and they must be protected at all costs. Johnny does learn one great lesson. He can do anything his heart desires, and he likely will not pay a price for his misconduct. In fact, today he is often portrayed as the victim, a celebrity in his own right. Hence, lessons formed in childhood extend into adulthood in the areas of cheating, untrustworthiness, rudeness, disrespect, and aggressiveness toward others.

There are more effects that linger in the hearts of bullies. As this book is being readied for the press, riots are raging in the streets of many cities across our nation. Portland, Seattle, New York, and Kenosha are being destroyed. These riots are caused primarily by young people, bullies, who come from the background of a dysfunctional family, or who have been paid to stage violent unrest and chaos.

Many rioters have little or no understanding of the character traits of civility and decency toward others. They were not trained as children to respect anyone. Permissiveness, self-centeredness, greed, do-my-own-thing attitude, and absent parents are the emotional and social norms of this generation. It is no wonder riotous living erupts when children have few limitations placed on them. The adult-child is like a free-range steer being corralled. He wants to shake loose and run roughshod over anyone or anything in his path.

In our current time, there seems to be a select group of youth dedicated to disrupting society no matter the cost. They are being funded by groups and individuals to do just that – destroy any semblance of civility and peaceful cohabitation. It is extremely sad and discouraging to hear various news agencies report that young people are being led down a path of destruction and chaos by well-funded individuals or organizations like George Soros, Antifa, and Black Lives Matter. Their goal is to destroy our Republic. Keep in mind that the bullying behavior of many protestors is encouraged by disengaged parents and progressive, leftist teachers. "The apple doesn't fall far from the tree," and "what goes around, comes around" can be directly applied to these usurpers of peace and tranquility. They were permitted to display anti-societal actions as children or young adults, and these characteristics were carried into adulthood, much to the detriment of modern-day society. It will take a long time and much effort to remedy the problem – if it is at all possible. I believe it is. Jesus said, "With man this is impossible, but with God all things are possible" (Matthew 19:26).

Along with the Holy Scriptures, lessons can be learned from the rules of civility and politeness of George Washington, as well as the simple dictates of Miss Manners and Emily Post. Look for these guidelines in chapters nine and ten. We now dig deeper into the beginning of our civility death spiral – the sad, sickening Sixties.

# Chapter Five

# THE SAD SIXTIES– PERMISSIVENESS RUN AMOK

*"Truly you set them in slippery places; you make them fall to ruin, How they are destroyed in a moment, swept away utterly by terror."*

Psalm 75:18-19

I f we could document a clear turning point in the civility of people and the lifestyle of our nation, it would be the sad Sixties. There was a kaleidoscope of moral hues foisted on a benign public that had never been seen before. Conservative Christian values were challenged and threatened. The standards of the past, at least according to the new generations, were no longer valid. They felt that they needed to be liberated from the moral standards that stifled individual freedom of self-expression. They wanted to do their own thing, no matter the outcome. The decade of the Sixties ushered in a moral cancer that has grown into a consuming malignancy which has devastated the character of the American people.

For a downward moral change to occur in a society, some subterfuge must take place. At least, that seems to be the modus operandi of some. Change must creep in quietly so as not to disrupt everyday living and abruptly change people's lifestyles. A little change here, a little chink out of moral principles there, is no big deal, so they think. As these changes pile up, the paradigm of society takes on a different shade. However, the societal change of the Sixties came not as little bits here and there, but as several sledgehammer blows to our moral compass which is what made the consequences so devastating and long-term.

We will look at each of the items on the list below to see how each one contributed to the decline of the moral standard of the nation:

- news media
- hippies
- Woodstock
- National Organization for Women (NOW)
- abortion
- flag burning
- separation of church and state
- rejection of prayer, God, and the Bible

## NEWS MEDIA

The news media is one of the most powerful influencers to ever exist in American society. They are subtle, secretive, well-financed and controlled to produce an agenda of their choosing.

Prior to the Sixties, a transformation was taking place in the news media, which came to fruition in that decade. Newspapers, radio and TV stations, magazines, and book publishers were small, usually locally owned organizations. The moral high ground was established and protected by people of good character. Most editors and publishers lived and interacted within their communities. Ever so subtly, one by one, these hometown outlets were scarfed up by big conglomerates with their own agendas. These big city organizations introduced a drastic paradigm shift into small town communities. Though the local media promoted conservatism, the larger big boys pushed the message of liberalism.

In the 1950s and 1960s, small, independent newspapers and local radio/ TV stations were the common means of news and entertainment. Patriotism, respect for God and family, and uplifting values permeated the written and spoken word. If you lived at that time, and were alert, you noticed that something began to happen that put us on the pathway of rejecting the principles which had previously guided our great nation.

Those corporately owned, liberal-driven newspapers and radio/TV stations implemented a strategic plan for infiltrating middle-America with their leftist propaganda. Little by little, editorials in the papers and scenes on TV were changing from wholesome and uplifting to raunchy and degrading. Your relative in the newspaper office and your neighbor's voice over the airwaves were replaced by journalists and announcers who carried out the ideologies of those who rejected God's ways. Today, many of the local media outlets unashamedly promote the agendas of both leftists and progressives.

This transition hit us with a crushing force and has taken place steadily since the 1960s. The vast majority of communication markets today have surrendered God-fearing principles, patriotism, small government, and sanctity of life platforms. The mindset of leftists rests on government control of the people. We are now at a constitutional crisis that may never be overcome.

## HIPPIES

The sad Sixties brought more changes to America and its culture. A class of malcontents known as hippies came on the scene. These were young men and women protesting against any established norm of society. They were tuned out and turned off to anything resembling authority, parental guidance, and moral rightness.

Hippies created their own communes where free love prevailed, and drug abuse was embraced and popularized. There were no limits placed on the individual to prevent him or her from expressing and activating the basest of desires, particularly if they reeked of anti-establishment. It was a time of rebellion.

Free thinkers were most admired in this utopian environment. Once a thought is embraced and used repeatedly, a habit is formed. Once a habit is formed, a character is built. Once a character is built, a life is established. Many lives built in the era of the 1960s would not show any embarrassment from crude deeds, violent actions, or self-deprecating thoughts. The trait, or custom, of blushing at a morally reprehensible deed was laid to rest in the repetitive actions of hippies. Civility was dealt a severe blow.

Hippies sought freedom from all constraints. It was a revolution against the moral standards that held our society together. Once the initial barriers were chipped and pock-marked, the assault upon all standards would follow. If everyone is doing it, the moral ethic is cast in favor of mob rule. Research the lives of people such as Jimmy Hendrix or Janus Joplin to see examples of those who destroyed body, mind, and soul. They knew nothing of blushing. The mind can conjure up despicable acts fueled by a free-wheeling livelihood. This led the way down the slippery slope to today's moral quagmire in which we now live, and move, and have our being.

In *Living on the Devil's Doorstep*, Floyd McClung describes his work with Youth with a Mission (YWAM) to the hippie culture in Kabul, Afghanistan, and Amsterdam, Holland. He and his wife ministered to this population of young Europeans and Americans who traveled the Trail from Europe to India looking for enlightenment. He writes of their "desperate longing to find answers and an almost mystical idealism. For many the search they were on covered up a desperate loneliness and aching emptiness. These were the lost and lonely children of the sixties and early seventies" (17).

I think it is important to include here McClung's actual words describing the hippie culture and mindset since he and his family worked so closely with them. He writes:

> At the root of the heavy drug abuse, the sexual hedonism, and the pursuit of Eastern mysticism lay a profound sense of alienation from Western culture. The long hair and beads, the flowing hippy clothing and the loose, low-key, laid-back lifestyle were all symbols of their rejection of everything associated with the pressure-filled, materialistic society they saw as being life back home. They maintained they were retiring from the rat race, leaving aside all the hypocrisy and the puritanical values and pressures to conform and compete. They endeavored to leave behind the civil service, the M.A. and the Ph.D., the mortgage in the suburbs, the neat nuclear family, and the nine-to-five rut. By setting off on the Trail, they were leaving behind the Church— and the stale, empty lies that to them it perpetrated. Two stereotypes of Christianity seemed to dominate their thinking. One was the 'believer-as-hypocrite,' who gave lip service to Christ in the pew on Sunday but never really lived it. This Christian talked about love and morality but lived immorally, shaking the preacher's hand at the door on the way out of church and then roasting him as

assuredly as the chicken or lamb they enjoyed at home a little later. Then there was the other archetypal Christian—the 'disciple-as-fanatic.' This wild-eyed Bible-banger grabbed unsuspecting people by the lapels and force-fed them the gospel. He or she was full of dramatic answers and wonderful testimonies, but never had time to listen to the questions (34).

The hippie era of the 1960s was not a pretty situation, and people needed some good old-fashioned fetchin's up.

## WOODSTOCK

If merit badges could be given out to the counter-culture crowd of the 1960s, a badge inscribed with "Woodstock" would be the prize meritorious award. Participants in that event are still held in high esteem by collaborators and sympathizers. The twenty-year span of the 50s and the 60s was a revolutionary time. I use the word "revolutionary" as a perfect comparison to our American Revolutionary War. In both historical events, people were striving for freedom. The contrast lies in the motives and agenda for each. Our military revolution was to free people from the tyrannical rule of another country; freedom in the truest sense of the word. The Woodstock revolution was held to promote social, political, emotional, and moral freedom; freedom in the perverted sense.

In August 1969, more than 500,000 young people gathered on a 600-acre farm near Bethel, New York. They assembled to listen to rock music and promote their message of unity and peace; in reality, they were there to protest control. These hippies wanted all societal shackles thrown off. Their cry for freedom from boundaries was expressed through free love, alcohol and drug abuse, anti-government, anti-establishment, and anti-war demonstrations.

Most attendees of Woodstock had parents from a gentler era in which life was regulated by moral and civil standards – God and country. Constraint, regulations, standards, and boundaries were rejected by this new generation of Americans. They longed to vent their disapproval of mom and dad's culture. While they outwardly espoused peace, they were inwardly raging against anyone and anything that limited their desires. I think of the Apostle John's words in John 2:15-17:

> Do not love the world or the things in the world.
> If anyone loves the world, the love of the Father is
> not in him. For all that is in the world – the desires
> of the flesh and the desires of the eyes and pride of
> life – is not from the Father but is from the world.
> And the world is passing away along with its desires,
> but whoever does the will of God abides forever.

In the participants at Woodstock, one could view clearly the desires of the flesh in drug use, sexual promiscuity and the pride of life. Self-expression resulted in the rejection of all traditional values.

Woodstock exemplified the rising immorality of our nation. Woodstock served to expand the reach of a new way of living. We were fast entering a world of zero embarrassment over actions and behavior that should have caused us all to blush.

## NATIONAL ORGANIZATION FOR WOMEN (NOW)

The inclusion of NOW in this book may be questioned by many liberals, if they even sit down to read it. They may ask how NOW contributes to the idea of blushing. I use the word "blushing" to illustrate the kinds of actions in word and deed that should cause embarrassment to an individual or a group because of civil and moral offenses. NOW stands accused of such offenses.

Betty Friedan, Gene Boyer, Pauli Murray, and twenty-five other women founded the National Organization for Women in June 1966. The founders of this organization were seeking true equality for all women in America, as well as non-discrimination in all aspects of life. In their 1966 Statement of Purpose, Betty Friedan wrote: "The purpose of NOW is to take action to bring women into full participation in the mainstream of American society now, exercising all the privileges and responsibilities thereof in truly equal partnership with men." At that time, the founding members believed that the status of American women was rapidly declining. They organized to "break through the silken curtain of prejudice and discrimination against women" in all areas of American society, including government, industry, education, and the justice system. They believed that "it is no longer either necessary or possible for women to devote the greater part of their lives to child-rearing," effectively barring them "from equal professional and economic participation and advance." From our twenty-first century view, the early goals of NOW do not seem too radical, but in the 1960s this organization was shunned by many mainstream Americans.

Under the current leadership, NOW declares itself "a multi-issue, multi-strategy organization that takes a holistic approach to women's rights. Our priorities are winning economic equality and securing it with an amendment to the U.S. Constitution that will guarantee equal rights for women; championing abortion rights, reproductive freedom and other women's health issues; opposing racism; fighting bigotry against the LGBTQIA community; and ending violence against women."

Even though some of the present grassroots activism is for critically important issues like domestic violence, abuse, and trafficking, many of their views are in stark opposition to God's Word and the Christian belief system. Additionally, their aggressive and liberal tenets regarding homosexuality and abortion are extremely harmful to women (and men) physically, emotionally, spiritually, and socially.

NOW wants to educate the American public (Conservatives) on the adverse effects of homophobia, promote positive media images of the sexual and gender choice community, and secure marriage equality for people of all lifestyles.

Visit the National Organization for Women's website to view their "Dirty 100" list. This is a list of one hundred plaintiffs who are under attack by NOW for their stance on contraceptive coverage under company-sponsored health plans. American Family Association, Liberty University, Hobby Lobby, Dr. James Dobson, Little Sisters of the Poor, Tyndale House, and Wheaton College are just a few of the organizations who seek an exemption from the requirement to provide birth control for their employees, based on a burden to their religious liberty.

The members of NOW fiercely support the Supreme Court's decision for pro-choice in the 1973 *Roe v. Wade* case. Thus the act of abortion – the murder of unborn children – came into public view as a strong position of liberal proponents. This one court case has led to the murder of over sixty million babies.

The National Organization for Women boasts of proud supporters and advocates for the rights of women. What they are really sponsoring is the mass elimination of children; the overthrow of the biblical standard of marriage and family; and the rejection of any individual, organization, or state that opposes their core issues. This is NOW's legacy.

## <u>ABORTION</u>

Shhhh! Don't bring up this subject! It's already been settled by government decree, so just don't stir the waters.

That is the attitude of many. That is the position of pro-choice liberals. That is the mindset of millions of Americans. If they don't see it, it doesn't really happen. Besides, it is a woman's right to do with her body as she pleases. It is only a blob of tissue. It is an inconvenience. It was a mistake.

Yet, millions of dead babies testify that Americans are guilty of genocide. We have looked the other way and buried our heads in the sands of ignorance.

The people of our nation agonize over the mistreatment of a cat or dog. We go ballistic if a panda doesn't have enough eucalyptus leaves to munch on. We protest and create advertisements of naked humans wrapped in fur to highlight the fate of animals. We argue for the rights of butterflies and fungi to the extent that certain areas of land are sacred and untouchable. Burrowing owl habitats are hallowed.

We notice the murders rates in Chicago or New York, terrorist shootings, and cancer deaths. Recently, we have been quarantined and admonished repeatedly to wear a mask, social distance, and wash our hands. Numerous publications quote statistics on heart-related deaths, diabetes risks, and drug overdoses.

It makes my stomach turn and my whole face turn red when I look at the latest statistics for abortion rates in the United States. Abortion is murder! Kate Smith, writing for CBS News, informs us that the abortion rate is at a historic low. The news agency cited the Centers for Disease Control and Prevention who touted the fact that 2016 had the lowest number of abortions since 1969. How shameful that CNN reports the fact that the abortion rate decreased from 2015 to 2016. There were still murdered babies! Thousands of babies. According to CNN's November 2019 report, "Abortion Fast Facts," the following numbers of American, unborn children have been willfully put to death:

2016: 623,471
2015: 638,169

2014: 652,639
2013: 644,435
2012: 699,202
2011: 730,322
2010: 765,651
2009: 789,217
2008: 825,564
2007: 827,609
2006: 852,385
2000: 857,475
1995: 1,210,883
1990: 1,429,247
1985: 1,328,570
1980: 1,297,606

These figures, these statistics, these deaths are mind-boggling. However, some would say we are making progress. According to my calculations, abortion rates are diminishing from one baby murdered every twenty seconds in 1990 to one baby murdered every fifty seconds today. While you were reading this page, two sweet babies were dismembered or burned with saline solution and scraped out of existence.

In the eyes of NOW supporters and Planned Parenthood, unborn children are blobs of tissue to be disposed of at a woman's discretion. There was, and is, no embarrassment, shame, or blushing at the ending of an innocent baby's life. According to the law, it is a legal act. That doesn't make it right.

The ending of life inside the womb stems from the numbing of moral standards that separates caring humans from barbarians. Life is no longer considered sacred by these people.

Did you see any headlines in your local paper or any news alert on your phone or TV calling attention to this genocide? Very few tears are being shed by Americans. Very few heads are hung in shame. We have come a long way to be so insensitive about human life. The coverup is working according to plan. People are distracted from the horrors of child murder. Make it legal and people choose to just accept it as normal in American society. Out of sight, out of mind.

THIS CANNOT CONTINUE TO HAPPEN WITHOUT GOD'S JUDGMENT ON THOSE WHO CHAMPION FOR WOMEN'S REPRODUCTIVE RIGHTS – ABORTION. WOE TO THOSE WHO PARTICIPATE IN, CONDONE, OR SUPPORT THE MURDER OF CHILDREN. BEWARE!!!!

Read Leviticus 20:1-5 to see what God said to the nation of Israel about murdering their children. Psalm 139 is David's acknowledgement that God is the Creator of all and that He knows everything about us. Verses 13-16 are especially appropriate:

> For you formed my inward parts;
> You knitted me together in my mother's womb.
> I praise you, for I am fearfully and wonder-
> fully made.
> Wonderful are your works;
> my soul knows it very well.
> My frame was not hidden from you,
> when I was being made in secret,
> intricately woven in the depths of the earth.
> Your eyes saw my unformed substance;
> in your book were written, every one of them,
> the days that were formed for me,
> When as yet there was none of them.

In the book of Jeremiah, the Lord reminded the priest that his life mattered from before conception. "Before I formed you in the womb, I knew you; and before you were born I consecrated you…" (Jeremiah 1:5).

Let us pray that a better day is coming when innocent babies will have the right to life as our Heavenly Father intended.

## FLAG BURNING

As a new Air Force recruit, I took an oath to protect and defend the United States of America. I swore to uphold the Constitution with my very life. Associated with these pledges was the unspoken, but understood duty, to honor the flag of our country. That was a given. It should still be a given for any citizen of this great nation.

My love for Old Glory didn't start when I entered the Air Force. It started at home as we celebrated many Independence Days with fireworks, parades, and flags. It was emphasized in elementary school when we looked at our flag and pledged allegiance each and every morning before class. Sadly, the pledge was lost as I progressed into high school and beyond, only to be resurrected on special occasions honoring our great nation.

During the 1968 demonstrations against the Vietnam War, flags were burned in protest and federal protection laws followed.

The *United States Courts* website explains that in 1984, Gregory Johnson burned a flag outside the Republican National Convention in protest of President Ronald Reagan's policies. Flag burning has become a means of protest for many individuals dissatisfied with the actions of our government and the founding documents of our land. Legal battles, congressional debates, and proposed amendments have sought a resolution over the desecration of our national symbol and the issue of free speech.

Johnson was arrested, charged, and convicted with violating a Texas statute that prevented the destruction of a national symbol if that action was likely to incite anger in others. Johnson appealed, and the Supreme Court agreed to hear his case. The issue in this case was "whether flag burning constitutes 'symbolic speech' protected by the First Amendment." The ruling in *Texas v. Johnson* was affirmed because "freedom of speech protects actions that society may find very offensive, but society's outrage alone is not justification for suppressing free speech." So, flag burning has been given the green light. SAD!

Another attempt to propose a flag desecration law failed in 2006. The latest recommendation to revise the language of the amendment was supported by President Donald Trump in 2019. Legally, any legislation to punish flag burners is silenced, but it does not silence many who believe flag desecrators are a dishonor to all who have given their lives to protect the freedoms won for all citizens of the United States.

Growing up in a free country sometimes clouds our minds about the beautiful liberties with which we are blessed. Just ask those new citizens who have been persecuted in their homelands and who have come and sought asylum in the United States of America. They will profess, with tears in their eyes, that once they come under the jurisdiction of our beautiful flag, a peace and tranquility penetrate their very soul; they are safe and free. The United States flag is the emblem of, the promise of, the hope of, the assurance of, a secure future.

Flag burners are a disgrace to our country. They have never crawled on a battlefield and watched their buddies ripped apart with sizzling bullets. They have never flown through anti-aircraft flack and seen their compatriot's planes go down in flames. They have never buried their friends. They will never blush from their disgraceful action of flag burning because they were never taught better. Or could it simply be willful rebellion against authority and civility? They have no idea what it is like to live in an oppressive regime, and they have no idea what it is like to live without freedom and liberty. They have never lacked the benefits guaranteed to everyone who lives under that grand old flag. They are reprehensible, despicable, and traitors to America. Maybe they should find another country in which to live.

At a recent Veteran's Day celebration here in our community, I was asked to give a short speech. It wasn't the profound oration that many great men have made in the past, but the ending had a deep meaning for me. As all who were there that day stood looking up to Old Glory, waving above our heads, I ended my speech with George M. Cohan's old song "You're a Grand Old Flag":

> You're a grand old flag
> You're a high-flying flag
> And forever in peace may you wave
> You're the emblem of
> The land I love
> The home of the free and the brave
> Ev'ry heart [should beat] true
> Under red, white and blue
> Where there's never a boast or brag
> But, old acquaintance [will soon] be forgot
> [So, keep your eye focused on,
> keep your heart stayed on,
> keep your faith in America centered on]
> **THAT GRAND OLD FLAG**

Long may she wave!!!

## SEPARATION OF CHURCH AND STATE

The inclusion of church—Christian morals—into social legislation is of prime importance in keeping any society functioning above a chaotic mass of hoodlums.

Our founding fathers were so astute in making sure biblical principles were included in the establishment of our nation that they repeatedly referenced God or the Divine Creator in much of their correspondence and legislation. They were not hesitant nor were they ashamed to call upon God for guidance. They were not shy about being recognized as a Christian, a follower of Jesus. They did not blush when looking for divine intervention in times of national disasters. They cared little for political correctness. They knew that their "help comes from the LORD, who made heaven and earth" (Psalm 121:2).

A history lesson may be in order here for the origin of the phrase "separation of church and state." President Thomas Jefferson first used the separation of church and state phrase in 1802. He was responding to an 1801 letter from the Danbury Baptist Association in Connecticut. The Bill of Rights Institute states that "Jefferson did not address the subject of state-sponsored churches, but assured the congregation that the federal government could not interfere with their church or offer special favors to any particular sect." Jefferson confirmed to the Association that "their legislature should 'make no law respecting an establishment of religion, or prohibiting the free exercise thereof,' thus building a wall of separation between Church & State." An interesting bit of trivia according to the Institute is that this popular phrase is not actually in the Constitution, though many believe it to be (Jefferson).

It is clear from his letters that Jefferson was a religious man, and he affirmed that the government should not interfere in citizens' faith and worship. However, it has been construed to mean that religion should have no influence upon government and the decisions made by representatives of that government. The early colonists and patriots were fearful of a King George of England-style of government which would force all citizens to worship as the government dictated. That was Jefferson's premise. Modern-day scholars have reinterpreted his statement to say that religion and all of its tenants should not be inserted in any government trans-actions or laws.

I think an analogy of a check valve is appropriate to describe this wall of separation that Jefferson mentioned. A check valve is a tool which allows fluid or any substance to pass in only one direction. Jefferson could have used a *check valve* reference in place of the *wall* to describe the correlation to America's government and religion in stopping the flow of influence by the government on religion while still permitting the flow of influence of biblical, moral, and civil standards on government. A government without the principles of God's Holy Word is a government devoid of ethics, tolerance, justice, and care for its people. It is an embarrassment to civilized people who experience laws without compassion. It makes people bury their heads in shame when they are ruled by an intolerant government. Biblical principles should apply to our laws, but laws must not dictate to biblical persuasions.

This country was established on biblical principles and the freedom to worship in any way deemed desirable to the individual. Of this there is no debate. A glance at the beginning chapters of this book reveals the reading material used by all schoolchildren at the inception of our Republic. They are filled with Bible passages and Christian moral teachings. I ask the question, "If it was good for our forefathers, why is it not good for us?" The liberals' quick reply is that we have evolved into a more enlightened society. Really?

How sad for our Republic and our people that biblical prin-ciples have been removed from public view. Once these founda-tional principles guiding the moral compass of a nation are caged, the direction of that nation is lost to any philosophy or ideology popular to the masses. The nation will be led astray without God's guidance.

## REJECTION OF PRAYER, GOD, AND THE BIBLE

Our forefathers were very adamant to call on Divine intervention when establishing our Republic or when faced with a crisis beyond their understanding or control. They were not deterred from bowing their heads and seeking a Higher Power to help them out of seemingly impossible situations. What would have happened to our country if General George Washington had not called upon Divine guidance that frigid day of 1778 in Valley Forge, Pennsylvania? Tom Konecny enlightens us to something that President Ronald Reagan stated in 1982: "I said before that the most sublime picture in American history is of George Washington on his knees in the snow at Valley Forge. That image personifies a people who know that it's not enough to depend on our own courage and goodness. We must also seek help from God our father and preserver."

Today it is frowned upon, it is ridiculed, it is criticized by society, and especially by many of our government leaders, to even suggest we call for Divine guidance in times of need.

The vast majority of Americans believe in God. He is the same God our forefathers worshipped. He is the same God who is revealed in the Bible, and He is the same God who can still be reached in prayer. Through the efforts of a minority of anti-religious, anti-God, anti-Bible zealots, the majority is castigated as foisting their religion on the oppressed few. As a result, the staple of society has been expunged and we are left with a manufactured human moral code which usurps the God-given and ordained biblical code of decent living.

The very thought that a prayer at a football game could be construed as offensive, or the display of a Nativity scene on any property could be deemed infringement on someone's civil or religious rights, clearly shows the depth to which we have sunk to remove God from our everyday lives. That's not the worst of offenses when it comes to total and complete separation of all things religious from public view. There is one name, above all others, that literally drives non-believers to a point of total hysteria. That name is Jesus. That name evokes visions of rules, moral laws, and discipline which is unacceptable to them. It brings into focus a control over their lives which they have rejected and wish to deprive others from embracing. The mention of Jesus' name in conversations within the media is frowned upon and subject to being removed as being too controversial or provocative. This is how far we have sunk as a God-fearing nation. From society's perspective, it is permissible and applauded to praise Islam, Confucianism, Buddhism, Taoism, Shintoism, and a multitude of other "isms," but don't mention Jesus.

The 1960s were a festering time in our society. A 1962 Supreme Court decision delivered a severe blow to our nation's religious tradition. This case contributed to the downward spiral of moral degeneracy. The Court's verdict in *Engel v. Vitale* "held that official recitation of prayers in public schools violated the First Amendment's Establishment Clause."

The "Regent's Prayer…was used to open the school day in New York public schools for much of our nation's history. Students who did not wish to say it could choose to remain silent or stand outside the room and face no penalty." It went like this:

> Almighty God, we acknowledge our dependence upon Thee, and we beg Thy blessings upon us, our parents, our teachers and our Country.

The First Amendment had been added to the Constitution to keep the federal government from establishing a national religion. It is often used today to exclude religion from public schools and other government spaces. While the *Engel v. Vitale* ruling did not outlaw all prayer in public schools, it did prohibit schools (school employees) from dictating prayers and the requirement to say them.

The Hugo Black Supreme Court ruled six to one against mandatory public-school prayer. It was declared that the state of New York had officially approved religion even though the First Amendment prohibits government interference in religion. In 1963, in *Abington School District v. Schempp*, Bible reading was negated from public schools. Michael Waggoner explains:

> These two landmark Supreme Court decisions centered on the place of religion in public education and particularly the place of Protestantism, which had long been accepted as the given American faith tradition. Both decisions ultimately changed the face of American civil society, and in turn, helped usher in the last half-century of the culture wars.

There have been "Bible Wars" through the last several hundred years, and in the late 1800s the nation was engaged in debate on the "intersections of church, state, and education in an unprecedented manner." Waggoner mentions author Warren Nord who "argues that we must educate more broadly *about* religion in ways that engender connection and understanding to enable civil discourse, discourse that involves our most deeply held beliefs." Over the years, as the pendulum has swung from the side of religion in schools to the side of religion out of schools, there are those today who believe that "education about religion may be more widely accepted in our universities and our public schools" (qtd. in Waggoner).

With removal of mandated prayer time, Bible reading, and religion, the die was cast to further exclude God from public schools. The downward trend of moral sickness in our children accelerated, for a society cannot maintain a sense of moral awareness without it being taught continuously to the children of that society.

God was expunged from our schools by a minority of atheists and judges who could not fathom the deleterious effect their decision would have on America. Students could no longer hear the Ten Commandments, the sermon on the Mount, or the Golden Rule in the classroom. The moral compass which existed in our public school for hundreds of years was now broken. Today, it remains shattered, and we see the whole of society in a moral quagmire of ugliness and disrespect for each other. There is no blushing for any infringement of morality or manners.

Chapter Six

# TECHNOLOGY AND SOCIAL MEDIA

*"When words are many, transgression is not lacking, but whoever restrains his lips is prudent. The tongue of the righteous is choice silver; the heart of the wicked is of little worth. The lips of the righteous feed many, but fools die of lack of sense."*

Proverbs 10: 19-21

America is deeply entrenched in a technological marvel called social media. This cesspool often communicates men's and women's deepest depraved thoughts and moral deficiencies. Where once there was restraint on derogatory and evil discourse between people, now TV, movies, Instagram, Facebook, Twitter, texting, and other forms of technology are rife with all manner of anti-moral sentiments. The family-oriented days of *Leave it to Beaver, Mayberry,* and *The Partridge Family* are a thing of the past. They have been replaced with an ocean of obscene, pornographical-ly-laced, morally reprehensible, yet socially welcomed, line-up of movies, TV programs, and internet sensations.

I find it interesting that at least one writer of the eighteenth century was so concerned about immorality in the arts that he wrote a protest about it. Much like I am doing! Adler and van Doren refer to Jeremy Collier, a social media contributor in England. Collier wrote about what he viewed as obscenity (pornography) and the abuse of morals in English drama. Adler and van Doren noted that Collier's title, *A Short View of the Immorality and Profaneness of the English Stage, together with the Sense of Antiquity upon this Argument,* is much more pointed and blatant about the problem than we would find in print today (79).

Collier published his book in 1698. In his Introduction, he explains that he is going to prove his points by showing the misbehavior on stage in respect to morality and religion. His examples include smutty expressions, swearing, profaneness, abuse of the clergy, debauchery, and indecent language. He writes:

> The business of *Plays* is to recommend Virtue, and discountenance Vice; To shew the Uncertainty of Humane Greatness, the suddain [sic] Turns of Fate, and the Unhappy Conclusions of Violence and Injustice: 'Tis to expose the Singularities of Pride and Fancy, to make Folly and Falsehood contemptible...

Chapter 1 of "A Short View" contains Collier's view of the immodesty of the stage. He presents compelling arguments of what he has observed, as well as his reasons for objecting to the lewd displays.

> Young people particularly, should not entertain themselves with a Lewd Picture; especially when 'tis drawn by a Masterly Hand. For such a Liberty

may probably raise those Passions which can neither be discharged without Trouble, nor satisfyed
without a Crime: 'Tis not safe for a Man to trust his
Virtue too far, for fear it should give him the slip!... it
does in effect degrade Human Nature, sinks Reason
into Appetite, and breaks down the Distinctions
between Man and Beast. Goats and Monkeys if
they could speak, would express their Brutality in
such Language as This...Smuttiness is a Fault in
Behaviour as well as in Religion... Obscenity in any
Company is a rustick uncreditable Talent;... In this
respect the Stage is faulty to a Scandalous degree
of Nauseousness and Aggravation... (sec.1-2, 6-8)

His work could be written for twenty-first century consumption relating to the depravity currently being displayed through
technology and social media. I recommend reading Collier's book.
It is 300 years ahead of its time.

There has been a major paradigm shift in our society. That main
shift has been in communications between homo-sapiens (people).
While there still remains ample communication, the scope of the
dialogue has been immersed in verbiage once thought totally
vulgar and extremely rude. This new interaction has emerged
through the process which could be called repetitious (or rote)
recitation. In other words, it's repeating the same obscene words
or phrases across all forms of social media—written, spoken, or
visual. The obscene words are heard often, they become familiar
and mundane, and they are then repeated with regularity and ease.
The more one does it, the easier it becomes, and soon it becomes
a habit. Add to this the ineptitude of the communicator to bring
forth proper words because of poor education or peer pressures.

This can be easily seen in a brief review of technology and media over the past seventy-five years.

## MOVIES

The movie world, society, and families were shocked when Rhett Butler said to Scarlett that he didn't give a damn in *Gone with the Wind*. How could anything so crude and obscene be allowed on the movie screen? Yet, following that supposedly innocent little phrase has come an avalanche of profane-pornographic-based movies with linguistics that should scorch the very lining of the ear canal. Everybody is doing it, and doing it, and doing it in repetitious recitation, and no one even blushes at the vulgarity anymore.

Hollywood, the liberal media capital of the world, has paved the way in scenes of debauchery, vulgarity, and pornography. Little by little, word by word, scene by scene, they have pushed the envelope to the point of acceptability for obscene public viewing far beyond its limit. From their productions, a new standard of acceptability and tolerance has arisen. Once a phrase or word is repeated often enough it becomes a part of the individual and his or her vocabulary.

Consider the "F" word. Fifty years ago, this word could only be heard in back alleys or from some degenerate person of low degree. Now, it is in everyday language of even some gentile souls. This has happened because Hollywood pushed beyond the boundaries of moral acceptability so many times the censors became numb to its sound, and actually even promoted it. Their ears were anesthetized to the vulgarity of the word and to the objections of the public viewers who wanted some control on language that would be acceptable for human consumption. Now, anything goes, and movie-makers hold back no act, word or deed that may enhance profit. No one blushes at four-letter words anymore.

Most children are no longer sheltered from the verbal filth that invades their home environment. We have become insensitive to even the grossest of speech because we permit it and enter into it more times than not. Shame on us!

I could list countless popular movies that sear the senses of viewers. Where should we start? One movie, *The Wolf of Wall Street*, uses the "F" word five hundred and six times in the one hundred eighty minute running time. It is repeated so often that the viewer is left with a deep rut in the brain containing only that word; or, has the word become so commonplace that the repeated usage goes unnoticed? Children too young to even understand the meaning of the word, repeat it with the calmness of everyday conversation. Some parents even encourage the language by endorsing the child's mimicking behavior through "Haha! How cute!" without realizing the indelible mark this is making on the child's brain. I challenge you to listen carefully to the next few movies you watch. Take a paper and pen and note how many times foul words are used. List the instances of sexual innuendos and sexually explicit scenes. I think you will be shocked at what you see and hear!

Movies do leave a lasting impression with viewers. They are supposed to do that. But, where do we, as responsible individuals, whether old or young, draw the line between movies that degrade and those that build up character and moral standing? We have a responsibility to safeguard our children's minds. We should act responsibly, and protect our minds and the minds of our children from the vulgarities that parade though movie screens. The Apostle Paul writes, "...whatever is true, whatever is honorable, whatever is just, whatever is pure, whatever is lovely, whatever is commendable, if there is any excellence, if there is anything worthy of praise, think about these things" (Philippians 4:8). I think our minds and hearts have become numbed to obscenities that constantly pollute the tinsel-town films of modern-day America.

Some, but not enough, in Hollywood actually do get it. Actor Denzel Washington noted on Instagram in 2019, "With so many things coming back in style, I can't wait till loyalty and morals become the new trend again."

Who is to blame for the denigration of values that destroy the moral integrity of humankind? We can blame the industry in their quest for the almighty buck. There is in every accountable individual the process of choice. Movies can be rejected or turned off with a flick of the button. Unfortunately, the appetite of the public today has become insatiable for more immoral and violent movies, and there seems to be no desire to reject even the filthiest of films.

The adult and parental acceptance of unwholesome language and actions in movies and elsewhere is a prerequisite for our children to emulate. "Like father, like son" is an old cliché, but the truth is that adults lead the youth of our nation to accept and wallow in the vulgarities of movies by streaming them into the home environment without any regard to the moral destruction of innocent children. It doesn't help that even very young children have cell phones and access to filth. It is easy to hear sexual innuendoes in Disney and other well-liked films. Children become so accustomed and de-sensitized to the language and lewd scenes on the screen that it becomes ingrained in their everyday character. Further, these words become part of their common conversations, and the violent and sexual scenes are often played out in real life.

Followers of Jesus are reminded to "Train up a child in the way he should go; even when he is old he will not depart from it." (Proverbs 22:6) That is a blessed promise for parents who train their children in biblical standards. Think of the implication for those who allow the presence of moral garbage to infiltrate their lives and homes. Parental responsibility involves self-control of personal viewing habits, as well as regular monitoring of children's movie choices. It's okay to say no to your children. In fact, it is our responsibility and duty to deny some things from ourselves and our children. Resist those movies that are not wholesome and edifying for all.

## TELEVISION

Oh, how we love our telly. How we use it for a baby-sitter, for social interaction, for occupation of the mind, and for just vegging on a Friday night or lazy Sunday afternoon.

Over the past few years, it has become necessary to grade all television programs, similar to the movie rating system. The grading is so very liberal, and the programs are so foul, that many really are not fit for children or mixed company. We are a far cry from Uncle Milty's saying (*The Milton Berle Show*) "You'll get a shot in the head!" which, of course, was made in jest. Therein lies the rub.

Many parents are busy. Momma and daddy have work obligations, and so the kiddos are plopped down in front of the TV screen. Junior and Jane view whatever they please.

The TV is the baby-sitter.

The TV is the teacher.

The TV is the character builder.

Whatever comes on the screen from the liberal, leftist, perverted minds of Hollywood's icons, who don't care a whit for your child, are etched into your baby's mind and soul, never to be fully erased. Foul language, obscene actions and gestures, immoral characteristics, and promiscuous commercials and programs are marketed to your child. Over a period of time, there forms a habit. An unconscious acceptance of garbage as something normal turns into a destructive character trait. We are familiar with GIGO: garbage in, garbage out!

Which is worse? Movies or television?

Which is less venomous? A cobra or a rattlesnake?

Both movies and television seek to poison the moral standing of all who watch… and watch… and watch, until the capacity for prudent judgment and moral civility is impaired beyond fixing. Even worse is the sad fact that many people have the TV on all the time, whether watching or not, just to have noise in the house. Even when you are not watching, your subconscious picks up on what your ears are vaguely hearing. The continual swear words and innuendoes do still invade your mind. You begin accepting and repeating what should not be seen or heard by any moral and civil person.

Television often replaces family communication. Sadly, so much is replacing family connections and relationships. We just don't converse anymore. It is easier to sit in front of the screen and not engage in meaningful dialogue with those closest to you. Is it that difficult to understand that our children have a lack of communication skills due to the myriad of carefully designed images and suggestions transmitted by anonymous directors and producers in Hollywood?

## SOCIAL MEDIA

Now we come to the heart of our well-loved and all-consuming communications that know no boundaries. What is thought in a person's mind is revealed on the device's screen for all to see and read. Personal secrets are made public. Family problems are displayed for all to read and comment on. Political, moral, physical, marital, spiritual, and personal characteristics are laid out for public consumption, and even worse, public response. We seem to rely on how everyone else views our situation. We face peer pressure and ungodly influences from across the world when we post on Twitter, Facebook, texts, and other social mediums. We don't seem to mind that degrading and unsavory images are normal and acceptable on this platform. We don't blush at what we see anymore.

It is one thing when an adult views filth and receives disgusting pictures. And, yet, our children are exposed to everything we are. My granddaughter has received numerous random comments and suggestions from perverts. There is no escape, no way to avoid these unwelcome advances other than to totally disengage from social media. I blush when I realize what my grandchildren experience daily. Social media has always been a part of life for the younger generations, but now they must carefully weed through the trash just to communicate with friends and relatives. I once knew a kinder and more refined era.

To say that there is no good in these forms of communication is short sighted. Instant communication can be productive and rewarding. It can draw families together. I'm grateful that my daughter and son-in-law have been able to connect with their military sons across the country and world. In our days of global pandemic, schools and businesses have been able to operate using modern technological platforms such as Zoom. It is truly convenient to order groceries and meals through phone apps. Young people do employ brain power and expressive communication to some degree. However, social media can be just as addictive as drugs or alcohol. It is common to find in an average group of five people in a waiting room, that four of them will be on social media.

There is a far more serious offense that occurs in social media. It is the anti-confrontation syndrome, or anonymity protection, that is guaranteed by faceless humans. We seem to have no sense of civility when we are behind a device. We can say anything when there is little accountability and moral restriction in place. It becomes so much easier to bully. It becomes so much easier to participate in sexting. Many will say things on social media that they would not say when looking eye-to-eye with another person. In essence, people are de-humanized.

Very often social media users demonstrate great bravado and boldness when spewing obscene, derogatory, hurtful, and nasty language through a medium that imposes no limits. In-person interaction would probably produce some hesitation or change in the form and content of communication. But broadcasting into the ethereal space of social media provides an outlet for all means of poor behavior and character. Individuals are relieved of the need of ever saying "I'm sorry." The perpetrator has no compunction to swallow his or her words.

Spoken words are a picture of the inner person. They can destroy or edify. The golden apples throughout this book serve to highlight the beauty of appropriate and encouraging words found in Scripture. In the Holy Bible, James writes how difficult it is to tame the tongue. He writes that we can set a life on fire with our words. We can ruin someone with the deadly poison spewed from our tongue. We bless and curse from the same mouth. "My brothers, these things ought not to be." (James 3:10)

The invention of cell phones, iPods, iPads, and other devices have created zombie-like people who may develop a deformed neck from looking down into the screen twenty-four hours a day, seven days a week, 365 days a year. Children expect, and parents feel obligated, to pay for sophisticated phones for babies not old enough to drive, vote, or write. But they can play games, text, watch cartoons, listen to music, and learn a foreign language with their expensive toys! This goes back to the babysitting theory. Rather than engage children's minds in learning games and face-to-face interactions with parents, we can have them learning their letters and numbers via electronic devices.

You may detect some sarcasm in my words. At my age, I don't have much patience for the lack of attention by parents to steer their children to bigger and better knowledge and politeness. I remember playing games with my children when we took long road trips. They may have been simple punch-bug games, but they stimulated my children to observe the world around them and remain focused on what is real and beautiful. What we all would have missed by sticking our noses into a device.

How often have you seen only the tops of heads in restaurants, at ballgames, in the mall, and in a waiting room? These heads are bent, not in prayer, but to view the game screen or to text somebody out there in la-la land. I suggest that there ought to be better manners displayed and more politeness shown toward our fellow men and women. Most folks are even too busy on their phone to offer a seat to an elderly person, a pregnant woman, or a disabled individual. Little needs to be mentioned on the illegal and deadly practice of texting while driving.

So, what does all this have to do with blushing? A lot. People who carry on the habits described above will not grasp the fact that these acts themselves are disgraceful, rude, uncouth, irresponsible and void of etiquette.

We ought to blush. We used to blush, in the past.

But times have changed, and that is sad.

Etiquette is not taught to children anymore. Etiquette is no longer adhered to by adults. Etiquette is no longer approved of by corporate America.

I submit that the most crucial training is in the moral areas of a student's life. Moral study includes the importance of orderliness, cooperation, thoughtfulness, manners, hard work, and respect. These are valuable for all of life and transcend into adulthood. Oh, that we would get back to the teaching of moral standards. What kind and civil adults and children we would see in our homes, communities and nation.

They might even blush once in a while.

Chapter Seven

# SCHOOLS, SOCIETY, AND GOVERNMENT

*"Where there is no guidance, a people falls, but in an abundance of counselors there is safety."*

Proverbs 11:14

*"The rod and reproof give wisdom, but a child left to himself brings shame to his mother."*

Proverbs 29:15

*"By mere words a servant is not disciplined, for though he understands, he will not respond."*

Proverbs 29:19

*"When a land transgresses, it has many rulers, but with a man of understanding and knowledge, its stability will long continue."*

Proverbs 28:2

Trying to tie schools, society, and government together in one chapter is a daunting task. But it must be attempted because the three are inseparably entwined and together form the basis of what makes our nation function for good or evil. The principles espoused in our schools are carried into our society and government just as leaven is carried throughout bread. They cause a rise or fall. In our earlier chapters, evidence was presented regarding early American schools and the methods and materials that were used. It's time to look at the present in light of the past.

## SCHOOLS

What makes a good school and good teaching? Is it the computerized learning paraphernalia in our modern schools that teachers rely on? Is it the billions of dollars doled out to school districts for computers, hand-held devices, free meals, and lessons in diversity and inclusion? I sincerely doubt if any of these make a good school or good teaching. So, what does?

For some time now, our schools have been failing. That does not mean that all teachers have been failing to teach. We have some great teachers who care, but are hampered by Unions or government decrees.

Yes, there are bad teachers, just as there are bad doctors, bad drivers, and bad electricians. We can find disengaged, unmotivated, uncaring, under-equipped, and insensitive teachers in all levels of education. A few teachers take advantage of students, crossing moral and legal boundaries. We know of teachers who propagate their own moral and political agendas. Students are indoctrinated with more than academic knowledge. Some people really should not teach.

At the same time, there are really good teachers in our school systems. They gladly spend their own hard-earned money for classroom supplies. They take our kids to science fairs, music camps, and art museums. They not only teach academic subjects, but they also oversee sports teams, cheerleading, field trips, clubs, and fundraising events. They figure out ways to make impossible situations possible. They are heroes.

Other teachers want to do so much more but lack the time or finances to provide what our children need. Today's teachers have to provide their own and their students' supplies, teach regular and special needs kids in the same room, juggle multiple formats at the same time (in-person and online), and pacify parents who create Facebook groups to complain about their child's teacher. Teachers must learn to love kids yet keep physical and emotional distances. Teaches fear that the next school shooting will be in their class-room. Teachers are targeted by students, parents, and administration for expecting decorum, obedience, and completed homework.

Recently, I went to my sixty-fifth high school class reunion. Before going, I went back through my archives and retrieved my fifth-grade class pictures that were taken in 1941. What wonderful memories they brought back to me. I couldn't help but wonder what became of all those urchins from my class at Roosevelt Grade School. I do know that some of them went on to be doctors, law-yers, dentists, military officers, and engineers, like me. How is that possible? We had fifty-seven students in that fifth-grade class. According to modern school philosophy, any more than twelve to fifteen students is the limit for effective teaching. How, then, did those fifty-seven kids rise to be learned men and women, and go on to be part of the greatest generation?

Here is my explanation:

1) Discipline
2) Discipline
3) Discipline
4) Oh, did I mention discipline?

69

Now don't get me wrong. I agree that there really are other things besides discipline, such as:

- reading with comprehension

Explanation: The ability to respond to information contained in your reading text, from answering questions with answers contained in the text to interacting with implied ideas and formulating advanced new concepts to ponder and grapple. "The mind passes from understanding less to understanding more" (Adler and van Doren 8).

Repeat, repeat, repeat, ad infinitum. Distinguished scholars say that repetition doesn't involve critical thinking; therefore, repetition is not useful. But, they imply, asking for student opinions on global warming and gender issues is useful. My response to this is, how can children respond intelligently to such profound topics as world peace, racial equality, embracing complexity, and immigration without a foundation upon which to build? Most adults cannot even have a reasonable conversation about such topics. To be clear, I do think there should be conversations about these topics, but students should spend years building a foundation of knowledge, experience, research, and facts before attempting to forge into deep critical thinking themes.

How many fast-food cashiers can make change for ten dollars without the help of the cash register computer? Where is the critical thinking when you are waiting for your change from that ten dollar bill? Repeating multiplication tables or scientific formulas until you are sick of them may not involve critical thinking, but these facts certainly remain easily recalled years later when you need to make change or do your ciphers.

- legible handwriting

It seems to be the consensus of education administration that neat writing is a no-no because there is little need for handwriting in the modern technological age. All writing is done via computer, right? However, I believe that every now and then it is necessary to pick up a pen or pencil and scribble a note to someone or write a check. (Agh! I forgot! We don't write checks now; we pay for everything by card or automatic banking!) In some cases, it is wishful thinking that handwriting would be legible.

I am firmly convinced that legible handwriting is important in a person's life. There are two reasons. First, it displays an effort on the part of the individual that he or she has put forth a discipline in written communication to rise above hen scratching. Second, legible handwriting demonstrates pride in one's ability to perfect a pleasing and clear means of communication.

What happened to cursive writing? The most beautiful of all writing methods has been outdated, replaced, and undone in schools. There really are debates about whether cursive writing is important and worth being taught. Many kids today cannot read cursive, much less write it. So, scratch cursive out! Do away with it because we have transcended to a higher level of computerized correspondence.

But wait! Maybe there are some sound reasons to be able to write cursive. Not only does it demonstrate discipline and order in a person's life, but it also takes practice and time to perfect the skill of penmanship. The practice and time are often the deterrent for many in this hurried up world. I believe that scratching a note or writing your name in indistinguishable hieroglyphics is a sign of laziness and lack of personal respect of self.

- storytelling

Is this important? I think it is especially important for elementary school kiddos. Telling stories helps children increase their aural and verbal skills based on their comprehension levels. Think of the thrill of listening to Aesop's Fables. Each one always has a moral lesson to discuss. Think of Bible stories. Jesus' parables were lessons in story form. For thousands of years, cultural traditions and values have been passed from generation to generation through verbal storytelling.

As I think back to my early school days there at Roosevelt Grade School, storytelling was a special delight in my education. Each day the teacher would read a selection from some exciting story. Her actions and voice stimulated our visual and auditory lobes so that we were transported to a wonderful world away from the cares and detractions of life.

It was not an escape from reality, it was an unfolding of a new frontier upon which to set a goal or learn a new constructive characteristic of life. Storytime should be a requirement for public school students today. However, there must be careful selection of edifying stories by those who adhere to high moral standards.

- discipline

Back to this point. Keeping order, controlling chaos, preventing a melee, eliminating bullying, establishing peace, and cultivating a positive environment for learning are essential for fostering moral high ground. Many classrooms today lack these qualities. Since it is now against all sensibilities to render physical punishment in public schools, teachers suffer the ill effects of violence and abuse at the hands of students. We certainly don't want to emotionally upset a child today, so they say. What hogwash!

The biblical passages at the beginning of this chapter are tried and true. Where there is discipline, there is learning. Through learning, comes respect. That is education and civility to the fullest.

Probably the most detrimental organization to learning in our schools is the Teacher's Union. It has been infiltrated by socialistic leaning, anti-Christian, politically motivated, anti-family input, claiming that more money is needed for them to teach effectively. Even when government is pouring money into their coffers, and the state lotteries contributing billions of dollars, they still plead for more financial help.

How can this all be fixed? I'm glad you asked. Here are a few points to consider:

## 1. MORALITY:

Since the solid foundation of biblical morality has fallen away, it will take great effort to restore civility and deportment. The fact remains, when there is quality moral training to guide students to love one another, respect others, show kindness, put others first, and turn from a self-centered attitude, there is learning. Look at parochial schools and homeschools. Often for these students, grades are higher and civility is better. What more could we want?

## 2. CURRICULUM:

So much modernization has gone into teaching methods and curriculum changes that old methods of teaching have been assigned a place with the dinosaurs. Yet, these modern methods have all but failed in promoting positive role models and higher educational levels. Money is not the answer. New methods do not always work. Drew DeSilver, of the Pew Research Center, explains the 2015 data that clarifies U.S. students are about mid-way on the scale in science, mathematics, and reading, even falling behind some other advanced countries. Our focus needs to return to reading, writing, and 'rithmetic, along with P.E. and the arts so students are well- rounded and equipped for college and life.

## 3. PARENTAL INPUT:

Where, oh where, did the Parent Teacher Association (PTA) go? Another dinosaur? In the past, those two groups, parents and teachers, would cooperate for the betterment of all students. Parents would review curricula, discuss the effectiveness of teachers, and brainstorm ways of assisting children to learn. They would plan social activities and events for students, leaving the teacher to teach. At one time, parents and teachers checked all government- produced curricula for the information it disseminated. Today, schoolbooks are full of communistic, socialistic, evolutionary, amoral, un-American, God-less slander. Our young people are becoming totally devoid of patriotism and morality, and are emotionally and socially crippled. Parents must make every effort to be involved in their children's schools, going so far as to inspect all school materials in order to ensure our Republic is producing citizens that will protect, defend, and advance our nation. This is of highest priority.

## 4. MANNERS:

Once upon a time there was a high school course called Home Economics in which girls were taught to cook, set tables, keep house, sew, and learn manners. That kind of thinking disappeared with the Model T's. Today, no sensible Teacher's Union or School Board would permit such a degrading course to be foisted upon our young businesswomen-in-training. Obviously, it is ridiculous to saddle girls with such sexist dogma. First of all, that kind of training is a thing of the past; secondly, you can't single out girls for such a topic; and thirdly, girls are worth more than being mere housewives. Times have changed and the home environment is passé, so they say. Girls can be anything they want to be. Phooey, I say. No girl can be a dad. Not every girl can be six-feet tall. Not every girl can be a Marie Curie. But, nearly every girl and boy can be taught to be polite, have good manners, and respect others.

As the thought of a simple course in manners reverberates in our minds, the question rears its common-sense head. Why not? Why not set aside an hour or two per week in the classroom to teach good conduct, manners, and sociability – to girls and boys? It might even improve grades in other subjects.

## SOCIETY

Our society is broken. I recently came across the term "zymotic society." This perfectly describes America at this time – a society in a continuous state of ferment as reported in Adler and van Doren (293). Many people today lack the necessary skills to be a kind person. It is getting worse by the generation. From out of our schools come young people who were never taught civility. It wasn't even in the realm of significant interest. Schools focus on other subjects. Parents do not know how to broach civility with their children; perhaps because they don't have a clue how to teach something they don't practice themselves. Children from every strata of society come from broken homes and dysfunctional families. One-parent homes are common today. Daddy is missing, and momma works two or three jobs to make ends meet. Children are forced to grow up quickly, leaving home in the mornings on their own, and coming home after school as latch-key kids. Even in two-parent homes, tiny infants are placed in daycare so both parents can work. Who teaches character and morality to your children? Are you the primary investor in the training up of your child, or is some other person and their value system the strongest influence on your child? Think about it!

Many children know nothing about loving others because they have never experienced unconditional love. They have not been taught about the love of Jesus Christ. They don't know how to forgive because they have never been taught about confession for wrongdoing, and they don't know what it all means. They know nothing about cooperation because they have been left alone to fend for themselves. Their mindset is "Do it to others before they do it to me." They do not know basic humility which would soften disagreements with others.

The people of our society are influenced by the things we hear, see, experience, and permit to enter our minds. The old saying "Let your conscience be your guide" is dangerous. Our consciences are tainted from conception, and our surroundings can be disastrous if we have poor examples from parents, teachers, preachers, or friends.

How do we define conscience? *Webster's Dictionary* gives us this: "a knowledge or sense of right and wrong, with an urge to do right; moral judgment that opposes the violation of a previously recognized ethical principle and that leads to feelings of guilt if one violates such a principle." The guilt for doing wrong is demonstrated by a blushing of the cheeks.

A conscience can be trained. It can be influenced. It can be adjusted from good to bad or vice-versa. There is no doubt, a morally pleasing conscience starts in the home with loving, caring, and instructive parents. Children must be taught from infancy, and we must not rely on the schools to do it. Though there are good and loving teachers who care deeply for their students, the responsible party before God is YOU. And by you, I am referring primarily to fathers who are instructed in God's Word to teach their children the words of the Lord "talking of them when you are sitting in your house, and when you are walking by the way, and when you lie down, and when you rise. You shall write them on the doorposts of your house and on your gates, that your days and the days of your children may be multiplied." (Deuteronomy 11:19-21) Unfortunately, many fathers are nowhere to be found. Mothers must do the training, trying to sandwich it in between providing, nurturing, protecting, and loving on all of the children by herself. It is a monumental task.

As we continue to think about our society, it is of prime importance that we try to understand why we need to turn our country around. Many people are still striving to come to America for a better life. This nation is still the greatest country in the world, but, it ain't what it used to be. Our decline comes from the polarization of political parties, the liberalization of schools, and the failure of parents to obey the word of God. The above passage in Deuteronomy goes on to instruct us that God placed a blessing and a curse before the people of Israel. When we hold fast to His Word we know that the principles apply to us today just as they did in the days of long ago. So, God promised that if the people were careful to do all that He commanded–loving God, walking in all His ways, and holding fast to Him–then He would take care of them in the face of their enemies. He would provide a solid, safe place for them to dwell, and they would be free and strong. If they did not obey His commandments, they would be cursed and not receive His blessings.

His Word is still true today. When we, families and society, follow Him, He will bless our lives. When we turn away, He brings punishment and consequences.

Unless this rejection of God ways is corrected, our nation will continue to decline.

Let's now center our thoughts on the government of the United States of America.

# GOVERNMENT

Where better to start than with a quote from Mark Twain: "The only time we are safe is when Congress is not in session."

There was a time in the history of the United States when a government employee could say, "I'm from the government, and I'm here to help you," and you believed him or her. That is not the case today. Events of the past fifty years have proven that the members of government lack candor and trustworthiness. Representatives of the people are no longer representatives of the people. Most are representative of the almighty dollar or promises of goodies to come by hook or crook. Our so-called representatives go into office with little or no financial stability of their own. Yet after a few years, they are wealthy beyond belief as a result of the favors they have bestowed on supporters, and the goodies they get in return from their bestowments. All of this is done under the table, so the public cannot see nor call them to account for abusing the office in which they serve.

Here are some key areas in which we see abuses by government officials:

## 1. LYING:

One of the greatest attributes a person can exhibit is honesty. We want this to be prominent in our elected officials. It is so important when drafting laws as well as when investigating skullduggery in and out of government circles. In essence, people are born liars, so there has always been dishonesty among men. It seems, however, that there has been a boundary crossed by our government officials within the past fifty years or so. I see it manifested especially in the Democratic Party—those liberals, socialists, anarchists, and left-wingers. The attempted impeachment of President Donald Trump has opened up a view of our Congress that is both unbelievable and unsavory. It was difficult to watch the impeachment proceedings and observe, in my opinion, the blatant lying of Representatives Shift, Pelosi, Nadler, Demings, and Senator Schumer among others. I see this farce as the most flagrant abuse of power ever displayed in the hallowed halls of Congress.

It is vital to understand the theme of this book. I am attempting to stress the fact that people no longer blush at rude conduct, telling lies, or moral and civil rebellion. Who actually cared about the lies that were told by the witnesses and officials during government-sponsored trials and proceedings? Who cared about the lies perpetrated in the Kavanaugh hearing for the Supreme Court justice? Are there no reputable, honest, trustworthy, or civil representatives in Congress anymore? More importantly, are there any Christians among the members of the House and Senate?

The sad travesty revealed here seems to be that allegiance to the political party overshadows allegiance to Christ and His message of redemption. How have we sunk so low?

"Hallowed" is a wonderful word. It means to be made holy, to consecrate, to consider sacred. Once, the halls of Congress were considered holy. Honesty was easy to find in members of that Body. Remember George Washington? However, the commitment to holiness and honesty has been thrown away like discarded jewels on a rubbish heap. Both political parties are guilty. "The end justifies the means" seems to reign supreme.

As this book is being written, Attorney General William Barr has just been interrogated by the Judicial Committee of the House of Representatives. Chairman Nadler and other Democratic members have demonstrated one of the most egregious episodes of misconduct, verbal abuse, impoliteness, incivility, character assassination, and unseemly behavior ever displayed in public.

This is not the only case of overt hatred and dishonesty from our public officials; however, in our current national crisis, the real travesty is that no one is blushing or ashamed. Most of us will remember former President Bill Clinton who boldly, blatantly, unapologetically, and angrily declared on national television that he had no sexual encounter with Monica Lewinski. That was a proven lie that almost led to his impeachment. And can we forget Hillary Clinton's lies about Benghazi, her emails, and the Russian dossier? The Clinton's perfected the art of lying to the public they were elected to serve.

Lying is a direct violation of God's ninth commandment: "And you shall not bear false witness against your neighbor." (Deut. 5:20) Lying is not a new sin, but it is becoming more apparent in those who are charged with leading our country. Few people search for truth anymore. Who blushes anymore?

## 2. SEXUAL MISCONDUCT:

I know that this is an uncomfortable subject for some. I also know that this type of behavior is not exclusive to our government officials, but here is the point. Our nation's leaders should be held to a higher level of responsibility and accountability because they are leaders. They are examples to all who live under their authority. As the greatest country on earth, and a Christian founded nation, we set a standard for people around the world to follow.

Did you know that you pay for sexual harassment settlements for members of our government??

Lee, Serfaty, and Summers of CNN Politics report that from 1997-2017, a portion of seventeen million dollars has been paid out in sexual misconduct settlements perpetrated by our government officials. The money for payments does not come from individual congressional offices, but comes from a special fund in the Treasury. The 1995 law that set up the Office of Compliance also set up this fund.

If you can stomach the filth and depravity, visit the online report from the Associated Press which gives a list of "…90 state lawmakers who have faced public allegations or repercussions over sexual misconduct claims." And these are only since 2017!

Rumors and allegations of sexual misconduct by men in office extend across the aisle.

Democrat and Republican leaders are equally guilty. Alan Smith writes of accusations against our early Presidents Washington, Jefferson, Jackson, Harrison, Tyler, and Garfield ("15 other presidents"). In more recent years, Presidents Roosevelt, Eisenhower, Kennedy, Johnson, Bush, Clinton, and Trump have all been associated with sexual affairs and escapades.

Going beyond the presidency, Franken, Weiner, Conyers, Meehan, and Kihuen are just some familiar names from Congress who have resigned due to sexual allegations and charges. Women are a small minority of those accused of sexual crimes, but it does happen.

Whether or not each and every governmental leader accused of sexual misconduct actually did it, all of these acts bring shame to the highest public offices in our land. The stained character of each perpetrator is forever linked to his or her public career and private life. It's not only the accused and the victim that suffer, but the wives, children, and other family members are also affected by things beyond their control.

Typically, there has been no blushing displayed in any of these incidents. Our leaders have lost their moral compasses.

## 3. GRAFT AND CORRUPTION:

The old adage, "Absolute power, corrupts absolutely," is the by-line and theme by which many Washington legislators conduct their everyday lives. The history of American politics reveals assorted instances of public officials lining their pockets with easy money from unsuspecting tax payers and generous lobbyists. The governmental graft and corruption within our system of leadership is extensive and revolting.

Govtrack's statistics show us the types of documented misconduct in Congress since 1789. They include campaign and elections charges, sexual harassment and abuse, ethics violations, and bribery and corruption. ("Legislator Misconduct Database")

Again, the crimes committed by our government leaders are by both Republicans and Democrats. Alex Greer posted a list of some of the largest congressional scandals in our nation's history. They include money laundering, the Congressional Post Office Scandal, bootlegging, bribery, ethics violations, corruption, the Keating Five, illegal finances, Korea-gate, the Chappaquiddick Incident, physical assault, McCarthyism, the Banking Scandal, ABSCAM, and murder. Watergate, Benghazi, impeachment proceedings, cattle futures, campaign donations, Russian collusion, classified documents, and tax-payer-funded vacations are some recent examples of misconduct and corruption. There are hundreds, if not thousands, of cases that could be cited, but one thing is crystal clear, the moral standards of many of the men and women who are elected to represent the populace are shameful. Too many are in office simply to wield power and sweeten their own coffers while the getting is good.

In October 2020, Pastor Ed Litton of Redemption Church near Mobile, Alabama, preached a sermon on how Christians are to live in light of political and governmental crisis. First, he reminds us that we are to be submissive to authority, those in power, our governmental leaders. Second, we are to have a kingdom mindset, that the Gospel should be our highest priority. And third, Christians are to engage with, not disengage from, the chaos of our times. Using Romans 13:11-14 as his text, Litton explains that in this letter, the Apostle Paul tells Christians to "...cast off the works of darkness and put on the armor of light. Let us walk properly as in the daytime, not in orgies and drunkenness, not in sexual immorality and sensuality, not in quarreling and jealousy."

The first section in verse 13, orgies (revelry) and drunkenness, refers to public spectacles.

Litton states that drunken people form a movement that creates disturbances. This movement harms people and destroys property. It is also clear that these are public offenses and outward signs of evil. We, as Christians, are not to get involved in this type of behavior. Our government officials should not be involved in them either.

The second section, sexual immorality (lewdness) and sensuality (lust), are often private or secret offenses. Litton states that in some Bibles, the word "sensuality" in verse 13 is translated debauchery, the inability to feel shame. "The absence of shame is dangerous to a culture. If you feel shame about something you have done, that's the Holy Spirit trying to help you be restored to the Lord. Shame is something that some people try to protect their children from; in fact, some kind of shame we all need to experience to learn the lessons of life. The absence of shame is dangerous."

The third section, quarreling (strife) and jealousy (envy), involve the heart and mind. These can be grudges against someone else, which hits close to the heart of many of us. "It is somehow beginning to cause discord in your community, in your family; it's fighting, it's jealousy ... murmuring, disunity, rumors, half-truths, and flat out lies have no place on the lips or the heart of a follower of Jesus Christ," Litton remarks. And, I proclaim it should have no part in the lives of our elected.

The early Christians lived in a difficult time with Caligula as Roman Emperor; and yet, Paul told them to pay their taxes, give respect, and give honor to whom it is owed. Litton referenced Tim Kellor's comments about the early church's civil involvement in their communities and in their government. Kellor breaks it down into five elements. The early church was:

1. multi-racial and multi-ethnic
2. highly committed to caring for the poor and marginalized
3. non-retaliatory, marked by a commitment to forgiveness
4. strongly and practically against abortion and infanticide
5. revolutionary regarding the ethics of sex

Litton commented, "Neither of [our governmental] party's has number three. And what we're watching on television is the sad reality of retaliation, anger, unforgiveness, bitterness, terrible words being used, attacks, personal vendettas..."

If the modern church would follow these five areas, through prayer, we could turn our world upside down. Our schools, society, and government could be transformed into places of peace. No blushing needed.

# Chapter Eight

# PROTESTS, RIOTS, AND ANARCHY

*"Young people who obey the law are wise; those with wild friends bring shame to their parents."*

Proverbs 28:7 NLT

The inclusion of this chapter, in a book about blushing, is very much needed. In 2020, one of the strangest and most trying years in history – other than the war years, our nation teeters on the brink of anarchy. First, we struggled through the attempted impeachment of President Donald Trump. Then, the COVID-19 pandemic began sweeping through our neighborhoods. We watched the murder of George Floyd and the subsequent unrest afterward. Finally, we had an election that further added anger, dissention, and ugliness to the populace.

There are many reasons for protesting, whether peaceful or aggressive. An honest evaluation is necessary to determine where peaceful protests (civility) end and anarchy begins. It is not difficult to determine the difference. One way protests a person, action, or law in a reasonable, civil manner; the other way destroys people, places, and things.

As we observe the recent riots and destructive marches, it is revealing to see that all the cities engaged in violence are Democratic controlled. All the leaders instructed their law enforcement organizations to stand down. In so doing, they permitted riots and destruction of businesses, small and large. It could have been avoided had they called on the President of the United States to send in military help, as he did in Kenosha, Wisconsin, and peace would have resulted. Yet, they chose chaos over peace. WHY? Simply because they wanted to disturb the election year as much as possible and placate to the far-left agenda. Also, those who were arrested for destruction of property or abusing those law enforcement officials who arrested them, were given a get-out-of-jail-free card from far-left millionaires supporting the anarchy.

The focus of this book remains: There is no blushing in our country anymore. People who participate in destructive riots head the list of non-blushing, unapologetic, and disgraceful individuals who probably never said "I'm sorry," in their lives.

To examine each of the activities listed in the title of this chapter is essential so as to determine the moral and ethical value of each.

## PROTESTS AND RIOTS

When there is a blatant abuse of justice, law, and order in a country, moral ruin and exploitation of human rights occur. We see a nation ruled by tyrants.

The people of the United States understand the value of peaceful protest, though many protests are not peaceful. Protests in this country include the Boston Tea Party of 1773 over British oppression; slavery and anti-slavery riots and rebellions during the early nineteenth century; labor and industry riots and looting, and racial justice marches and protests in the twentieth century; and, of course the current rash of disturbances. We know from our history classes that Susan B. Anthony and her Suffragettes marched for equal voting rights for women. We know that Martin Luther King, Jr. marched peacefully to free his people from racial bondage and give them equal rights as unrestricted citizens of the nation. The list goes on and on.

How do we determine what a just and respectful protest is? Some rebellions have been calm and civilized marches or verbal discourse. Other protests have erupted in absolute chaos, destruction, and anarchy.

Of the countless protests in the history of the United Sates, it is impossible to designate which one was the most meaningful. The truth is, a protest is meaningful to different people, at different times, for different reasons, under different circumstances. My goal is to key in on the demonstrations of this era in American history since they are fresh in our minds and part of our everyday conversation and television news shows.

Many current protests are centered on the alleged abuses perpetrated by law enforcement officers. Reporters and journalists focus on bad cops, but fail miserably to highlight the work of good cops. There are bad cops. There are bad pastors. There are bad lawyers. There are bad political representatives. There are bad people. They are all around us. We must not reject one because of the other. As the saying goes, "Don't throw the baby out with the bath water."

In early 2020, George Floyd was handcuffed and killed by an officer of the law. Protests arose due to this abuse of power. Mr. Floyd was murdered in front of our eyes, thanks to television coverage. As investigators presented facts of the case, they revealed that the policeman responsible for this crime had at least twelve citations for abuse of power or transgressions of protocol and policy. There was no explanation for the situations surrounding the citations. This, of course, is troubling to all who march for, and want, true justice for all. Subsequent inquiries into the officer's citations revealed that there is no policy for the release of information to the public about the conduct of any police officer, no matter how troubling or offensive their misdeeds may be. Hence, peaceful protests erupt into unruly demonstrations and riots in order to focus attention on policies that protect the guilty.

Many of the protestors simply ask for law enforcement agencies to honestly review the deportment of any of their offending officers periodically. Too bad they can't apply these requests to congressional people. They want complaints to be evaluated carefully and openly to determine if they are valid or submitted viciously in order to destroy the officers' character and reputation. This can only be done through an unbiased panel permitted to view all the facts and witnesses. If accusations and charges are proven true beyond reasonable doubt, the officer must be prosecuted.

There is another side to this story which involves the emotional make-up of an officer. Most law enforcement agencies include some emotional training for all members. They are trained to keep their cool. However, the officers' jobs are not easy, and they are expected to stay calm and polite in the face of all types of evil, both physical and verbal, up to threats of death. After a shift, they are to remove themselves from this negative environment and go home and try to make an emotional change into a person of peace, kindness, joy, patience, and love with his or her spouse and children. These officers are not quite superhumans, although many really seem to be.

Over a period of time, many officers become calloused in their actions on the job and they tend to give what they are receiving from those who abuse them. There are many reasons for this. Some police officers grow up in a dysfunctional, non-loving home environment. This often happens in homes with an absent or abusive father. They have little control over their habits as a young person and sometimes these bad habits stay with them through life. Others may have lived in a neighborhood riddled with crime, drugs, gangs, and violence which molded their character of retaliation against abuse. Still others become so desensitized and hardened as a result of the crime and violence they witnessed, they find no way to relieve the pressure and stress.

A few of our finest do fail, once in a while. So do pastors, priests, and presidents; and so do we, and all should be held to account. I sincerely believe that 99.9% of all law enforcement officers are honest, hardworking, reputable, non-abusive, caring purveyors of protection to the general public. I salute them all.

When an offending characteristic becomes evident, and citations are given to an officer, it must be carefully evaluated by those in charge to determine the cause of concern. Repeated violations should not be allowed to continue; corrective actions for flagrant violations should be made public so all can see the scope of the corrective action. There must be active oversight and accountability even to those who serve us as protectors of the peace.

Peaceful protests must never be curtailed. During this year, many peaceful protests have transformed into something more aggressive and with evil intent. Two organizations in particular, require closer scrutiny. Were the recent demonstrations peaceful protests that ended in riots, or were they riots plain and simple? Let's take an honest look at the doctrines that guide Black Lives Matter and Antifa. Perhaps we can see what guides their activities to reveal some underlying motives for riots and not peaceful protests.

## BLACK LIVES MATTER (BLM)

#BlackLivesMatter was founded in 2013 by three black women; Alicia Garza, Opal Tometi, and Patrisse Cullors in response to the acquittal of Trayvon Martin's killer, George Zimmerman. It has grown to an international movement today.

Months ago, it was easy to find the foundational guiding principles of the BLM movement. They were horrendous and frightening.

Once people began to join the organization as a sign of solidarity with black people, attention was drawn to BLM's platform. Now, the original statements have been reduced to something somewhat more palatable for the public. Even with the watering down of its statements, BLM leaders want to "dismantle cis-gender privilege and uplift Black trans folk, especially Black trans women." They "are committed to fostering a queer-affirming network. When we gather, we do so with the intention of freeing ourselves from the tight grip of heteronormative thinking or, rather, the belief that all in the world are heterosexual unless s/he or they disclose otherwise." They want to dismantle the patriarchal system. They want to do away with male-centeredness, and they want to engage "comrades" in their work.

Olivastro and Gonzalez report the reasons for BLM's revision of history. They explain that there has been a drop in support because people do not like what they see as the agenda and ideology of this organization. BLM is a movement that is trying to divide the American public rather than unite it.

In response to the ongoing social issues, concerned and compassionate people across America have connected to the published slogans of BLM in their fight for life, liberty, and the pursuit of happiness for all – especially African-Americans who have been wronged through the centuries, and are being wronged today. However, choosing to support the publicized agenda of BLM without knowing all that this group stands for is irresponsible and reckless.

Yaron Steinbuch of the *New York Post* reports that co-founder Patrisse Cullors claims to be a trained Marxist. She and her fellow organizers trained with a group which "uses grassroots organization to 'focus on Black and Latino communities with deep historical ties to the long history of anti-colonial, anti-imperialist, pro-communist resistance to the US empire.'" According to the article, this training ground for BLM founders "also expresses its appreciation for the work of the US Communist Party, 'especially Black communists,' as well as its support for 'the great work of the Black Panther Party, the American Indian Movement, Young Lords, Brown Berets, and the great revolutionary rainbow experiments of the 1970s.'" Cullors' mentor, Eric Mann, was connected to a radical group "led by Bill Ayers and Bernadine Dohrn, who called for 'direct action' over civil disobedience, seeking the overthrow of the US government. In 1969, the FBI classified the group as a domestic terror organization."

Roland Warren's 2016 analysis/opinion piece in *The Washington Times* confirms that the press, celebrities, and politicians, including former President Obama, have jumped on the bandwagon in support of #BLM, many of whom have not even visited their website. The twelve Guiding Principles were provided on BLM's website which can easily be Googled.

However, if you objectively read these principles, you will quickly notice that most of them have nothing to do with the issues facing the black community, and, certainly, not the black men and boys that the group has used as 'martyrs' to gain a national voice. Moreover, as you read the principles, you will not find a single reference to black men and boys, except for 'trans brothers,' which are men who want to be considered women. Also, it is clear that the Black Lives Matter ideology sees no role for black men, especially not as husbands and fathers.

Warren continues by writing that BLM founders want to disrupt "the Western-prescribed nuclear family structure" where there are only "mothers" and "parents." He asserts that BLM has no use for black men other than to use them as media props to promote the agenda that actually excludes and degrades them.

If you recall, when #BLM recently became prominent, many were shouting "Black Lives Matter!" Woe to those who countered with "All Lives Matter!" They were ridiculed and chastised for not focusing on black lives; after all, it was the blacks who were being persecuted.

The guiding principles promoted by Black Lives Matter fall short from protecting the lives of their black brothers and sons on the streets of Chicago and New York. There are very few uprisings, riots, marches, or outrages over black citizens killed in these cities and the senseless slaughter of young, defenseless black children who have been hit by stray bullets from the gun of another black person. Yet, all manner of chaos breaks loose when a white police officer, defending his own life, kills a black man. This is prejudicial and racist on the part of Black Lives Matter. They forget their own, and seemingly count them less than nothing in their quest to key in on specific concerns of propaganda. This is a disgrace to the black community and a ploy to disguise their true goal of pitting blacks against whites to bring chaos, incivility, and disunity between the races.

Warren, a black man, encourages people to deeply consider the truth before joining and promoting this organization. Garza, Tometi, Cullors, and their fellow Marxists don't value all black lives, they don't value men, they don't appreciate the traditional family, they don't respect America, and they are wrong. The BLM movement is anti-government, anti-Constitution, anti-free speech, anti-peaceful demonstrations, and anti-civil.

## ANTIFA

This movement began in Europe in the 1960s, reached our nation by the end of the 1970s, and has had the express purpose of harassing white supremacists and right-wing extremists.

In "Who are Antifa," The *Anti-Defamation League* reports that Antifa, short for anti-fascist, came to prominence in America in 2017. Primarily, antifa is characterized, not as a unified organization, but as a loose collection of groups and people who aggressively confront "what they believe to be authoritarian movements and groups."

When antifa arrive at a protest, rally, or demonstration, they regularly bring violence and conflict. "Most antifa come from the anarchist movement or from the far left, though since the 2016 presidential election, some people with more mainstream political backgrounds have also joined their ranks." With their belief "in active, aggressive opposition to far right-wing movement," antifa is now also targeting conservatives and supporters of President Trump.

They are anti-fascist, anti-police, and anti-racist thugs. They move violently to shut down free speech seen on many college campuses today. They smash windows in businesses and set fires to establishments under the guise of protecting others. They are masked, secretive, and destructive. Their tactics include "throwing projectiles, including bricks, crowbars, homemade slingshots, metal chains, water bottles, and balloons filled with urine and feces. They have deployed noxious gases, pushed through police barricades, and attempted to exploit any perceived weakness in law enforcement presence. Away from rallies, they also engage in 'doxxing,' exposing their adversaries' identities, addresses, jobs and other private information. This can lead to their opponents being harassed or losing their jobs, among other consequences."

America was founded on the idea of peaceful protests. Antifa demonstrations are far from peaceful as seen from the burning of businesses, destroying property, injuring those too weak to defend themselves, and usurping peaceful protests of civil demonstrators. There is not one ounce of civility in their actions. They do not retreat from their destructive campaign to squelch the freedom of speech and human rights. They do not blush over their actions and never will. They are the epitome of evil.

In December 2019, Gabriel Nadales of *The Hill*, reported that Antifa "doesn't stand *for* anything, only *against* whatever it decides to define as fascist." Nadales, a former Antifa activist, expressly supports Voltaire's proclamation "I disapprove of what you say, but I will defend to the death your right to say it" (qtd. in Nadales). Sadly, this is not the Antifa way, and they adhere to their methodology of violence and mayhem toward any and all they deem warrants their abuse. They will never, nor do they know, how to blush for their nefarious deeds.

Recently, President Donald Trump has recommended that Antifa be classified as a domestic terrorist organization. This would be a blessing to those whose businesses have been demolished and those whose lives have been destroyed. From sea to shining sea, destruction by Antifa hoodlums has wreaked havoc with honest working-class people.

## ANARCHY

Anarchy is defined as "the complete absence of government; political disorder and violence; lawlessness" ("Anarchy"). #BLM and Antifa's activities revolve around rejection of authority. Many believe that those who march with BLM and Antifa are anarchists who oppose local or national democratic rules and regulations, and in particular, as established in our Constitution. Anarchists decry government authority and control on all lives. They want a free reign of society unrestricted with archaic laws of control on a person's right to free expression.

Where there is uncontrolled evil and destruction, there is an absence of civility and good manners. Individuals associated with riotous living and deleterious characteristics are such people. This includes all those connected to Antifa. They want "to destroy our democratic republic and establish an authoritarian regime where dissent is crushed and beaten into submission" (Nadales).

Federal Law 18 U.S. Code Section 2385 Advocating overthrow of Government, made this type of federal crime punishable by fine, up to twenty years in prison, and/or ineligible for employment by the United States for five years afterward. A 1969 U.S. Supreme Court case, *Brandenburg v. Ohio*, held that "Speech that supports law-breaking or violence in general is protected by the First Amendment unless it directly encourages people to take an unlawful action immediately." That reduction of criminalization literally paves the way for BLM and Antifa to initiate acts of violence and destruction, while hiding behind the language of the court case. BLM and Antifa members, whose riotous acts devastated people, places, and things, will never be held responsible for their actions, and they will never pay a price for their uncivil, corrupt lifestyles. To them, anarchy is a way of life.

They will never blush or be ashamed of their actions because they are indoctrinated that way, or they are paid to act that way. May God have mercy on them, and may God protect the peaceful protestors and the majority of the American people who protest lawfully. May we all pray to the Lord for a better tomorrow, a kinder and more loving populace.

# Chapter Nine

# GEORGE WASHINGTON'S RULES OF CIVILITY AND DECENT BEHAVIOR

*Let the wise hear and increase in learning, and the one who understands obtain guidance."*

Proverbs 1:5

*"The fear of the LORD is the beginning of knowledge; fools despise wisdom and instruction."*

Proverbs 1:7

George Washington's little book, *Rules of Civility & Decent Behavior in Company and Conversation*, is a true gem. It ranks equal to, or surpasses, other books on how to conduct a person's daily life. It contains Washington's personal rules of civility–not suggestions, but rules to follow in order to be a civil and decent person.

Michael McKinney explains that before Washington was sixteen years of age, he was challenged to copy 110 maxims (rules) for proper behavior. These rules were ancient, stemming from Jesuit scholars of the sixteenth century. It is not precisely known how these rules came to be in the Commonwealth of Virginia, but it is known that they were circulated in the New World colonies and embodied into the character of our first president.

If we were to read these French Jesuit rules, we may think they are quaint and outdated. But McKinney writes;

> … they reflect a focus that is increasingly difficult to find. The rules have in common a focus on other people rather than the narrow focus of our own self-interests that we find so prevalent today. Fussy or not, they represent more than just manners. They are the small sacrifices that we should all be willing to make for the good of all and the sake of living together. These rules proclaim our respect for others and in turn give us the gift of self-respect and heightened self-esteem.

What kind of person is a civil person?

A search of the 1828 Noah Webster *American Dictionary of the English Language* gives us some synonyms for understanding the meaning and intent of the word "civil." These synonyms include civilized, courteous, gentle, obliging, well-bred, affable, and kind. A civil person has refinement of manners and is not savage or wild. The 2020 edition of *Webster's New World College Dictionary* remains solid in describing civil as polite, courteous, chivalrous, and gallant. Both dictionaries refer to the private rights of a citizen which are lawful and orderly.

A look at several synonyms sheds light on what a civil person's character may encompass.

- courteous: implies actively considerate and dignified politeness (working hard to show politeness)
- chivalrous: observant of the forms required from good breeding, high-minded and self-sacrificing acts of concern for others' well-being.
- gallant: spirited and dashing behavior and ornate expressions of courtesy
- polite: polish of speech and manners, emphasizing cordiality

This is the type of person whom President Washington admired. These are the qualities that he believed were imperative for decent people to practice. He worked to acquire civil characteristics in his own life. These are the qualities President Washington was advising people to emulate.

A civil person not only adheres to man-made laws of etiquette, but he or she also strives to practice the biblical model of polite and obedient behavior. King Solomon's Book of Proverbs is filled with wise sayings and godly counsel designed to make a person pleasing in the sight of God and man.

A few of the Proverbs relate to President Washington's lifestyle and obedience to his own father. In Proverbs 13:1 we read: "A wise son hears his father's instruction, but a scoffer does not listen to rebuke." Also, Proverbs 15:20: "A wise son makes a glad father, but a foolish man despises his mother."

These two simple proverbs typify the kind of teachings a father would give to his son or a teacher to a pupil. It is precisely what Washington's father endowed him with. Washington's life was a blessing to his father and mother, and to America. It would be a foolish man who would ignore his mother's advice and lose the proper pathway to successful living and service. Washington was a hero, not only in warfare, but in daily living with exemplary deportment.

In the content of this book, I have discussed numerous instances of wicked plans and evil actions by individuals and organizations. From hardened, habitual criminals to athlete-scholars to religious leaders, men and women run toward evil. Most of us can name political leaders who wield power and stand on a platform of beliefs that go against every idea of decency we hold dear. We have seen corruption in the White House. We have seen abuse in the churches. We have seen ugliness in our homes.

Where has the sign of respect gone? As we look at our society today, we are confronted with disrespect from people of all walks of life. From government, to schools, to offices, to homes — respect is lacking. It seems like the trend is that the more vocal one is, the louder one talks, the more that person becomes a vocal bully.

You can watch disrespect demonstrated on the professional ball fields as players reject the Pledge of Allegiance. You can hear caustic remarks on television talk shows as so-called journalists verbally rip apart people they disagree with. People running for political office, at all levels, do not act decently toward one another, instead lowering themselves to the actions of a bully or name-caller. Local school board meetings and community gatherings are not exempt from conflict. Children have learned well. All you have to do is listen carefully when you are out and about to hear how children speak to their parents.

But here is the problem. Adult leaders and authority figures are so busy with everyday happenings that we don't make the time to train our younger generation. Civility takes a back seat to the TV, the cell phone, and work. Arrogance, disrespect, vocal abusiveness, crudeness, and a myriad of other bad traits erupt from the mouths of young and old alike. The abnormal becomes normal in their character and demeanor, and our society degrades to caveman manners. If you don't believe that, just observe our government leaders and see the disrespect between political parties and individuals. It is egregious.

As we think about the attributes of our first president, he was a man who not only talked the talk, but also walked the talk. Throughout his life, Washington was known as a modest, courteous, and truthful person. The story of George and the cherry tree used to be common reading for children, partly because it was a good story with an honorable character, but also because it was a way to demonstrate the quality of honesty for children to emulate. Do some research on your own to discover his rules of good behavior.

To understand his manners, deportment, and rules of civility let us look at a few edicts from Washington's 110 maxims of proper behavior. McKinney states that the original spelling and structure are unchanged, so permit me to add some interpretive comments for each Rule:

## Rule No. 1:

"Every Action done in Company, ought to be with Some Sign of Respect, to those that are Present." Simply put, everything you do or say in public ought to be done in a respectful manner. That's very good advice for people today.

## Rule No. 5:

"If you Cough, Sneeze, Sigh, or Yawn, do it not Loud but Privately; and Speak not in your Yawning, but put Your handkerchief or Hand before your face and turn aside." This is excellent and healthy advice. Don't let your driveling (saliva flow from mouth or mucus from the nose) be spread to others. Cover up!

## Rule No. 15:

"Keep your Nails clean and Short, also your Hands and Teeth Clean yet without Showing any great Concern for them." *Cleanliness is next to godliness* is a statement recorded by John Wesley in 1778, but also found in Babylonian and Hebrew texts. ("Cleanliness") We're not to make a big fuss about this – just do it habitually.

## Rule No. 21:

"Reproach none for the infirmities of Nature, nor Delight to Put them that have in mind thereof." Washington was far ahead of his time by insisting on respecting anyone with infirmities – whether physical or mental. He might have requested to have handicap parking places for carriages of people with disabilities.

## Rule No. 36:

"Artificers [a skilled worker] & Persons of low Degree ought not to use many ceremonies to Lords, or Others of high Degree but Respect and highly Honor them, and those of high Degree ought to treat them with affability & Courtesy, without Arrogance." Washington knew the Golden Rule, as related by Jesus in Matthew 7:12 when He said, "Do unto others as you would have others do unto you." Washington's rule was to treat others with respect. That would be good for everyone to follow today.

## Rule No. 48:

"Wherein you reprove Another be unblameable yourself; for example is more prevalent than Precepts." Washington was an example to others when he reproved them for their misdeeds. He reminds his readers to check that their character and actions are above reproach.

## Rule No. 49:

"Use no Reproachful Language against any one neither Curse nor Revile." This one's simple – don't cuss anybody out.

## Rule No. 100:

"Cleanse not your teeth with the table cloth napkin, fork, or knife; but if others do it, let it be done without a peep to them." Don't be a slob. Use a toothpick to get food from between teeth. Hopefully they had them in the 18th century.

AND FINALLY

## Rule No. 108:

"When you speak of God or his attributes, let it be seriously & with reverence. Honor & obey your natural parents although they be poor." This is a great Rule that characterizes George Washington's lifestyle of reverence to God and obedience to his parents. It is a directive that reflects back to the First Commandment – "You shall have no other gods before me." (Exodus 20.3), and the Fifth Commandment – "Honor your father and your mother." (Exodus 20.12) What a great influence he had on America and her people. He personified Christian civility, love, compassion, and morality.

George Washington's rules of civility cover just a small portion of etiquette. In the next chapter, we will look at a more modern approach on etiquette and manners.

One of the most memorable speeches ever given was President Washington's Farewell Address as he left office. James Clark of *Task & Purpose* reveals seven excerpts from that speech which show the manners, respect, concern, and love he had for others and our nation. These characteristics ought to be drilled into the hearts and minds of every American.

A united nation benefits all states.

President Washington states that all "citizens, by birth or choice, ...must always exalt the just pride of patriotism..." They (the citizens) must reject self-centeredness and discrimination. Our independence and liberty are, and always will be, a joint effort. The love of Union must supersede the love of state or self.

There is a difference between strength of arms and a large military establishment.

President Washington supported the absolute need for a strong military to protect the country from foreign intervention. However, he warned that too much power of a military force could be "particularly hostile to republican liberty."

Both hostilities and relationship with foreign nations should be approached with care.

"The nation which indulges toward another an habitual hatred or an habitual fondness is in some degree a slave." Washington warns that this may lead to opportunities to "tamper with domestic factions, to practice the arts of seduction, to mislead public opinion, to influence or awe the public councils." This may doom America to be a "satellite" of another nation.

A unified nation is far stronger than an alliance of independent states.

The T.E.A.M. acronym – Together Every one Achieves More, echoes the long-established maxim from Aristotle: "The whole is greater than the sum of its parts." This is Washington's plea to the new union and to those challenged to preserve it for posterity. "To the efficacy and permanency of your Union, a government for the whole is indispensable."

An educated nation is an enlightened and moral one.
"Promote then, as an object of primary importance, institutions for the general diffusion of knowledge ...that public opinion should be enlightened." He suggests this nation should be morally presentable, also.

Power must be tempered by humility.
President Washington apologizes for any errors in his life or in service to America. He humbly beseeches the Almighty to forgive any evil he has committed. Truly he was showing his exceptional character of humbleness for which he was so noted.

[Returning to Private Life]
The President was anticipating the sweet enjoyment of a private life, "good laws under a free government," and a "happy reward" for his meritorious work on "mutual cares, labors, and dangers."

While these statements from Washington do not specifically point to manners or civility, they do show his demeanor in his overwhelming love for country. This author contends that this attribute can only be displayed by a moral and forthright individual whose underlying character is founded on a sterling decorum.

Finally, Erickson writes on his blog, *What would the world be like,* that "George Washington had a strong moral character and he was considered a person of impeccable character." Erickson provides a testimony from Abigail Adams (wife of the second president) that is worth its weight in gold. She writes: "He is polite with dignity, affable without formality, distant without haughtiness, grave without austerity, modest, wise, and good." Washington's lofty reputation was upheld by his actions. As Henry Lee (father of Robert E. Lee) put it, he was "First in war, first in peace, and first in the hearts of his countrymen." Would that we could each attain such heights of civility and teach them to our children.

# Chapter Ten

# ETIQUETTE, EMILY POST, AND MISS MANNERS

*"Be not deceived, evil communications corrupt good manners."*

1 Corinthians 15:33 KJV

God's Word—the Bible—is the greatest book ever written. In it can be found numerous instructions concerning civility, respect, and honor. Jesus is the greatest instructor regarding human relationships.

Consider His Golden Rule found in Matthew 7:12: "So whatever you wish that others would do to you do also to them." Note another command from the Master found in John 13:34-35: "... love one another: just as I have loved you, you also are to love one another. By this all people will know that you are my disciples, if you have love for one another."

I have written much about the erosion of good manners in American society. As General Douglas McArthur stated: "Old soldiers never die, they just fade away." Perhaps good American manners have just faded away because they are seldom used anymore and are not taught to the younger set. What you don't use, you lose.

In this book, we recognized that schools don't have etiquette classes on their schedules anymore. Some of us from the 1940s or 1950s may remember those classes which trained young people in good manners.

When was the last time you saw a man remove his hat when entering a building? Have you ever seen a man wear a hat into a church building and keep it on in the sanctuary? I was taught to remove my hat in the presence of ladies, as a sign of respect for the flag, and when I entered a building. These are good manners — in a community of respect and decency.

How many times do you see people chomping on gum – in the schoolroom, the church, during a conversation? I was taught to chew quietly and calmly. I was taught to throw my gum into the wastebasket before class, and certainly before church services. This was a demonstration of good manners—in my day.

How often do you see the intent to place girls before boys in line? Practicing good manners means girls before boys, not because girls are better or more important, but because it is a sign of respect and deference.

Do you ever see men or younger people give up their seats to older people or women, in a waiting room, on a bus, at a concert or ballgame? Do you ever see people hold the elevator door for others? Do you ever see people go out of their way to open doors, carry heavy items, or let others pass in front? Do you see good manners from drivers? Likely, you can clearly recall a recent scene of road rage.

Do any infractions of the aforementioned behaviors make you blush? They ought to! My daughter taught her children the acronym J.O.Y. – Jesus, Others, Yourself. Make Jesus first priority in your life, and then put others before yourself to show good manners.

Trying to pinpoint the origins of the departing of good manners would be extremely difficult. When good manners exit, churlish behavior enters, and that's our society today. Like it or not. Live with it if you wish. Count me out. I don't want to settle for less. I want to see a change in our families, our communities, and our nation. Keep reading; I'm going to get to our chapter on what to do about our problem.

Some of us may recall the reams of instructions on manners that came from the pens of Emily Post and Miss Manners. Actually, who are Emily Post and Miss Manners, and, why should you care what they say?

Emily Post was an aristocrat and a person of affluence. Born in 1872, she made an indelible mark on society in the area of manners. If you are younger than 50 years of age, you probably have little or no perception of her contribution to etiquette, conduct, and manners. In the 1920s and 1930s, she was a giant in the realm of polite company. Emily was a successful writer and traveling correspondent. In 1922, *Etiquette: In Society, In Business, In Politics and At Home*, was published and hit the bestseller list. "The phrase 'according to Emily Post' soon entered our language as the final word on the subject of social conduct."

Five generations later, *The Emily Post Institute* online:

> ...maintains and evolves the standards of etiquette that Emily Post established with her seminal book Etiquette in 1922. According to the Posts, though times have changed, the principles of good manners remain constant. Above all, manners are a sensitive awareness of the feeling of others. Being considerate, respectful, and honest is more important than knowing which fork to use. Whether it's a handshake or a fist bump, it's the underlying sincerity and good intentions of the action that matter most.

Miss Manners, whose real name is Judith Martin, was born in 1938. She was a journalist and etiquette authority. Miss Manners' Facebook page describes her as "the pioneer mother of today's civility movement." In 1978, Martin started writing an advice column in which she answered etiquette questions from readers:

> Readers send Miss Manners not only their table and party questions, but those involving the more complicated aspects of life – romance, work, family relationships, child-rearing, death – as well as philosophical and moral dilemmas. ...Her subject was for years dismissed as an archaic frill to be dispensed with by a world that was much too busy to trifle with such niceties. Yet serving as the language and currency of civility, etiquette reduces those inevitable frictions of everyday life that, unchecked, are increasingly erupting into the outbursts of private and public violence so readily evident in road rage, drop-of-the-hat lawsuits, fractured families and other unwelcome byproducts of a manners-free existence. These unpleasant developments have bred a nationwide call from academics, politicians, writers of all stripes and the public at large for a return to common courtesy.

Many people may say these two ladies are old-fashioned and their advice is not germane for today. I agree they are old-fashioned, but they are also good-fashioned and desperately needed in our chaotic, rude, uncivil world.

Etiquette and good manners ought to make a difference because there is a need, a craving, a calling to be a more gentile society, and maybe create a blush or two.

Have you observed modern young people and their interactions with others? Some of our youngsters are absolutely polite, kind, considerate, generous, civil, gracious, unselfish, and patriotic. Others are not. It is often impossible to get young or old to look up from their cell phone. Trying to get their attention usually results in a half-hearted "Huh?" "What do you want?" or "No problem." There is a problem, and it lies in the lack of education about good manners and civility.

The call for etiquette is not a new fad. *The Maxims of Ptah-Hotep* was written around 2375 B.C. Thirty-seven topics of moral advice and proverbs for young men came from this Egyptian vizier. He extolled humility, graciousness, kindness, good manners, leadership, self-control, moderation, and obedience. He described how to raise a good son and how to be kind to your wife. Good stuff back in B.C. and still applicable for us in A.D.

John Daly provides a short history on the evolution of etiquette from Ptah-Hotep to modern writers. Daly references an Italian who, in A.D. 1200, was one of the earliest writers on civility. Around A.D. 1290, a Milanese monk wrote a book on proper table manners. He reminded his readers not to be lazy at the table, not to gulp food or drink, not to pick the teeth, and not to talk with the mouth full. In the 1600s and 1700s the French royals learned some rules of etiquette from King Louis XIV. One of them was: Keep off the Grass!

Even with historical and modern etiquette resources available to the public, a number of Americans certainly don't practice good manners and civility. Apparently, they have had no fetchin's up. Where would they have learned them? At home? – Too busy. In school? – More important subjects to teach. In church? – It's not the church's responsibility. On Facebook or Twitter? – Heaven forbid. From peers? – Not likely.

It is said that "As goes our youth, so goes our society." From the 1960s we have seen an exponential increase in impoliteness, rudeness, incivility, and belligerence from all ages. When we adopted the attitude of "Do unto others before they can do it to me," our citizens began a new standard of poor civility which we wallow in today. It shows its ugly head in our government leaders, our schools, our communities, our places of worship, and our homes. No one is exempt. There is no shame. There is no remorse. There is no BLUSHING!!

A solution is available for this decline in civility, but it won't come easy. Good manners must be reintroduced into our homes, schools, and churches. God commands parents to teach biblical truths and positive character qualities to their children. Homeschoolers must be intentional about adding character training into their daily schedules. Headmasters and principals must choose to offer classes on good manners, civility, and patriotism. Pastors, church staff, Sunday School teachers, and children's ministers should emphasize Jesus' teachings on uplifting and edifying qualities, with greater enthusiasm and consistency.

As we ponder the effects of rudeness and incivility, it should come as no surprise that some people experience personal pain, anxiety, heartache, self-destructive thoughts, substance abuse, and introvert tendencies. An old childish saying applies here: "Sticks and stones may break my bones, but words will never hurt me." This is as false as the day is long. Words can hurt. Nasty, cutting, profane, and vindictive words do hurt. They hurt terribly, and they can linger in the mind for years. They may not bruise bones, but they certainly have the capacity for bruising and wounding the spirit. Many have come away from a tongue lashing with a churning and upset stomach seeking Alka-Seltzer for relief. How sad that we treat each other this way. Worse, we see no blushing at all from this practice.

# Chapter Eleven

# LAGNAIPPE: COMMON SENSE

*"For the LORD gives wisdom; from his mouth come knowledge and understanding; he stores up sound wisdom for the upright; ... and watching over the way of his saints."*
Proverbs 2:6-8

*"Wisdom is the principal thing; therefore get wisdom. And in all your getting, get understanding."*
Proverbs 4:7 NKJV

I wonder why common sense is so hard to find.

It doesn't seem to be in the thoughts and words of Alexandria Ocasio-Cortez ("AOC") (D-NY). She stated that unemployment is low because everyone has two jobs. She also believes that a seventeen- year-old can purchase an assault weapon. She asked, at one point, whether it was okay to still have children because of the issue of climate change. Most of you will remember Ocasio-Cortez's comments about the Green New Deal in which cows and airplanes will be eliminated to get to net-zero carbon emissions.

It is probably unfair of me to criticize AOC for her lack of common sense since this is a book about civility and good manners. But, I wish to help her as she proposes methods of ridding the environment of cow flatulence. As a chemical engineer, I have developed a formula for a cow feed and want to recommend it to her. It will reduce cow gas substantially. The feed is called Flatulent Free Fodder, or 3F fodder for short.

The 3F fodder is composed of just three ingredients. It is one third grain, one third hay, and one third Gas-X. Gas-X is the secret substance that will reduce the production of flatulence that cows eliminate daily by a magnitude of twenty, or thereabouts. Researchers inform us that cows produce between 160 and 320 liters per day of methane gas. So, there you are AOC; if you hurry, you can get a patent on the 3F fodder and we will all breathe healthier. Good luck, and you're welcome.

Several other issues from 2020 that highlight the absence of common sense include an elementary student who was suspended for having a gun in school despite the fact that the child was in virtual school, the gun was a BB gun, and he simply moved it out of the way of a younger sibling. A shared lack of common sense involved the mom who ignored the mask mandate and was tased by a large police officer. She was at her son's outdoor football game and she was sitting by herself.

Despite the faults and failures of certain leaders in our society, there are still many intelligent people found throughout governmental circles. They have great intellectual power and wisdom beyond compare. However, in their striving for brain knowledge, some failed to get common sense. *Webster's* defines common sense as: ordinary good sense or sound practical judgment. As we look at the behavior of politicians, parents, preachers, and the public, we must stop a moment and ask: Where did common sense go?

Years ago, there was a story about the demise of Common Sense that has been noted as an obituary in the London Times. From John P. McDonald III of *The Times Union* it goes like this:

THE DEATH OF COMMON SENSE

Today we mourn the passing of a beloved old friend, Common Sense, who has been with us for many years. No one knows for sure how old he was, since his birth records were long ago lost in bureaucratic red tape. He will be remembered as having cultivated such valuable lessons as:

- Knowing when to come in out of the rain;
- Why the early bird gets the worm;
- Life isn't always fair;
- And maybe it was my fault.

Common Sense lived by simple, sound financial policies (don't spend more than you can earn) and reliable strategies (adults, not children, are in charge).

His health began to deteriorate rapidly when well-intentioned but overbearing regulations were set in place. Reports of a 6-year-old boy charged with sexual harassment for kissing a classmate; teens suspended from school for using mouthwash after lunch; and a teacher fired for reprimanding an unruly student, only worsened his condition.

Common Sense lost ground when parents attacked teachers for doing the job that they themselves had failed to do in disciplining their unruly children.

It declined even further when schools were required to get parental consent to administer sun lotion or an aspirin to a student, but would not inform parents when a student became pregnant and wanted to have an abortion.

Common Sense lost the will to live as the churches became businesses, and criminals received better treatment than their victims.

Common Sense took a beating when you couldn't defend yourself from a burglar in your own home, and the burglar could sue you for assault.

Common Sense finally gave up the will to live after a woman failed to realize that a steaming cup of coffee was hot. She spilled a little in her lap and was promptly awarded a huge settlement.

Common Sense was preceded in death

- by his parents, Truth and Trust,
- by his wife, Discretion,
- by his daughter, Responsibility,
- by his son, Reason.

He is survived by his 5 stepbrothers:

- I Know My Rights
- I Want It Now
- Someone Else Is To Blame
- I'm A Victim
- Pay me for Doing Nothing

Not many attended his funeral because so few realized he was gone (qtd. in McDonald).

As we leave this treatise on common sense, I thought I would create and add a whimsical, but somewhat serious, limerick.

### *Ode to the Death of Common Sense*

There once was a nation of common-sense folk,
Which grew and prospered as a great mighty oak,
But they lost common sense,
And failed in defense,
'Gainst those who stole freedom and gave us a yoke.
[RKP]

# Chapter Twelve

# FAMILY, FAITH, AND FUTURE

*"A Family that prays together stays together."*

Fr. Patrick Peyton

*"Be watchful, stand firm in the faith, act like men, be strong."*

1 Corinthians 16:13

*"Therefore do not be anxious about tomorrow, for tomorrow will be anxious for itself. Sufficient for the day is its own trouble."*

Matthew 6:34

My church's motto is "Faith, Family, Forever," and it has a powerful message. It inspires a positive outlook on life, and one that encourages our members to strive for God's best. Faith in Jesus Christ is essential for a successful life now and in the future. Every person has a need to belong, to have other people to lean on. The family is the backbone of any society. Family can be defined by more than just blood relatives. We sometimes count co-workers, close friends, or social groups as family. We are reminded that developing faith and family takes time.

## FAMILY

As we look around our society today, we see families in total disarray, living in dysfunction and disorder. Many are fatherless, powerless, spirit-less, and hopeless. The old saying, "As the family goes, so goes the nation, and so goes the whole world…" is so true. Families are falling apart and our nation is in decline. To save our nation requires the saving of our family unit. It has taken time for America to come to this point, and it will take time to restore values, priorities, and godly families.

Coming up during the Great Depression was difficult, not only on kids, but on parents, as well. Losing my mother when I was thirty days old nearly destroyed our family unit, but my dad would not give in or give up. He was counselled to give me and my three older siblings up for adoption or send us to a children's home. He would not do it. My grandmother did her best, with the help of my older sister; and finally, a step-mother joined us. Our family was stabilized, but still very fragile. The most important aspect of our making it was my loving, Christian dad and step-mother.

Several key traits were evident in my home, holding us together in the midst of sorrow and loss.

**1. Self-sacrifice** – It would have been so easy for my dad to give up when my mom died. He could have looked around at four sad, lost faces and given in to unsolicited advice. What could a single dad do with four little ones during the Depression? There was no question, he had to work. For our health, safety, and security, Dad could have given us to another home.

It is not unusual today to see that many individuals in families promote a self-centered attitude. Parents are often selfish, wanting what will please their desires and dreams. Mom wants a sleeker, faster car with all the bells and whistles because Mary Beth down the road just got a new Mercedes. Mom feels that she deserves a vacation for herself so she can be pampered and kid-free for a week. Dad wants a new and bigger boat so he can get away in style and impress his buddies. He enjoys those business trips to relax from home responsibility and just enjoy himself. The kids want the newest phone that downloads an app or game faster than what their friends have. Life becomes a theme song: "It's all about Me." Parents and children have little remorse about being selfish, and they show no embarrassment or blushing tendencies.

My sweet dad gave of himself so that our family could remain intact. He made it work. His example has impacted my life in ways I never expected. I look back now and understand what he sacrificed so that he could keep us four children. I had a happy, fulfilled life growing up. We were poor, but because of my dad's self-less spirit, we had each other. He put his God first, taking us to church and teaching us biblical integrity by word and action. He made family the second priority after God, giving of himself to raise us in peace and joy.

**2. Generosity** – "God loves a cheerful giver," so Paul tells us in 2 Corinthians 9:7. We take that to mean we should be cheerful givers of money. Yes, we should, but there are other things we need to give: help, kindness, attention, a smile, a hug, a listening ear, sympathy, time, and cheer.

Generosity in my family was easy to see. I just looked at my daddy – Asa Parsons. I watched him go without shoes to buy us kids one simple Christmas present. I saw him neglect his health so we could have food to eat. I watched as he mended his worn-out shoes with half-soles because he had spent what little money he made each week at Goodyear on my winter coat. His generosity and self-sacrifice knew no bounds in our family unit.

Greed is destructive. When a person has an intense desire to accumulate things for personal benefit, other people get caught in the crosshairs. Greed tears families apart, pitting husband against wife, children against parents, and so on. What starts in the family often erupts into our society, nation, and world. There is so little embarrassment or shame about the level of greed we see all around us. It's not okay. Hang your head in blushing shame you who covet your neighbor's goods, your neighbor's spouse, your neighbor's property, or your neighbor's success.

**3. Compassion**—We see compassion in the actions of Jesus. He cared for the woman caught in adultery. He wept over his friend's death. He loved Zacchaeus, Matthew, Peter, and Saul.

My daddy's compassion was evident at the drop of a tear. There was no greater soothing medicine than his calloused hand on my forehead when I was nauseous or feverish. There were hugs for a broken arm, tenderness when removing tape that encased that arm. There was encouragement and compassion over a lost sports game. "Better luck next time," he soothed. This all sounds so simple, but for a young boy it was the epitome of fatherly compassion.

In a self-focused family, there is little room for compassion. Too many parents neglect the needs of their children. Children, as well as adults, are under constant stress and pressure in our rat-race society. Family members try to handle pressure-cooker issues alone, and parents don't often consider, or remember, the struggles of childhood and teenage years. Children need physical contact with their parents. Children need understanding and encouragement when faced with peer pressure, sibling rivalry, and hormonal changes. Concerned adults need to show compassion and care for neglected and abused children in their communities.

Compassion extends to senior citizens, as well. When we have pity for, and express concern for, the sufferings of others, we demonstrate compassion. Caught up in work, pleasure, status, and self is no environment of compassion.

**4. Love** – the Apostle Peter wrote that "… love covers a multitude of sins" (1 Peter 4:8). With true love in our hearts, we can forgive the mistakes and wrongs of those closest to us. We can only love others "because he first loved us" (1 John 4:19). Jesus' command is "…that you love one another as I have loved you" (John 15:12).

How did Jesus love us? He gave His life for us. The unsaved will not understand the grace and love of God. A big problem within many families is ignorance of true love as defined by God through Jesus Christ.

Read on to see how the lack of love relates to blushing and embarrassment.

As we journey through life, some relationships come and go. They prosper and wane. Sometimes the loss of a loved one ignites a regret that we did not look after that person as we should have. We lament that we neglected a parent, sibling, or friend, and now it is too late. We failed to show love, care, concern, patience, or attention.

During times like these our hearts cry out, "Why didn't I love more?" I become embarrassed and hang my head in shame — I blush at my behavior. I wish I had another chance to make things different and love just a little bit more.

God's Word is so very rich in meaning when we read "Let love be genuine…" (Romans 12:9). That means without hypocrisy, insincerity, or fakeness. Love is more than skin-deep. Love in good times and bad. Love at all times.

Family love must be genuine, tenderhearted, sincere, all-encompassing, and generous. Then there will never be a need for embarrassment, blushing, or regret because "love never ends." (1 Corinthians 13:8)

My daddy never said to any of us kids "I love you." That might sound cold-hearted if it were not for the fact that he showed us those words by his actions. His love was guaranteed. It was steady and reliable. It was absolute. I experienced it, and I still rejoice in it long after his home-going.

## FAITH

Faith to many people is a nebulous word. Having faith in something is questionable when that something cannot be seen or touched. We are called on to have faith in things, people, processes, ideas, and a slew of other intangibles. People fail their faith test in many areas of life. Going it on their own is a way of life. Some fail to find the proper source of faith. Therefore, hope for a better tomorrow, hope for a better family, hope for a better lifestyle is never pursued and never found. It is not wrong to put the subject of faith in a book about civility and blushing because where there is no faith in biblical standards, life can be disappointing, embarrassing, and sad.

Faith has its roots in the family, but the family must be centered on a Power beyond human understanding. Faith is defined in the life of a young man, Tim Tebow, who demonstrated his faith before a watching and cruel nation. When told "don't do something," or "you can't do something," or "you shouldn't do something," Tebow realized these were the same people who didn't, wouldn't, and couldn't do <u>anything</u>. They lacked the faith to try. Don't listen to them, he said. Trying to do anything on your own is putting your faith in your own power. It never works well. We need faith in Someone we can trust, Someone who never fails.

That Someone is the Creator of the universe and the One who sustains, protects, provides, and brings redemption to a lost and dying world–Almighty God.

Second Corinthians 5:7: "for we walk by faith..." Every moment of every day we have faith, whether consciously or sub-consciously. We hope for the next minute of life. Our lives are held in His Hands. That is an awesome thought which should lead us to the conclusion that if He controls our very existence, we ought to let Him be the subject of our faith. As Creator and Sustainer of all things, our faith, our future, and our hope should rest in the One who will make all things good and right.

He can give us abundant life. Our faith has a resting place – in the grasp of the One who won't let go–Jesus Christ. When we place our faith and trust in Him, our future is secure and no embarrassment will be seen; we will not need to hang our heads in shame.

## FUTURE

In this chapter, family and faith have been discussed and evaluated. Now let's look at the word "future" and try to weave this into the theme of blushing. It may stretch our weaving ability, but it is necessary in order for us to understand how all these ingredients fit together on the grand journey of life.

Christians are fond of saying, "I don't know what my future holds, but I know Who holds my future." What does your future hold? Do you know? Are you confident about your future? Who holds your future? How does this connect to blushing?

Lots of people work very hard to have a successful future. They want to retire in comfort and live care-free. Some spend enormous amounts of money to get the best education money can buy. Some work from sun-up to sun-down to position themselves to have a good life. Along the way they forget, or maybe they never knew, how to get that good life. They knew how to make a living but could not understand how to make it a life. They did not seek a life that was meaningful, a life that was a blessing to others, a life that was pleasing to their Creator, or a life that would merit a lasting legacy. At the end, when life was slipping away, they lay on their death bed and shed tears of sorrow at their misconception of what a well-lived life looked like. No one ever taught them the true meaning of life. No family member, no church, and no school invested time and effort to share the Good News. Our world reels from this today. Only a return to the One who controls all lives and all futures will bring the cure for the sickness and sin of a dying world.

A safe, prosperous, and pleasant future is not guaranteed to any human. It is a blessing to have enough money to buy a secure retirement, but money doesn't always guarantee a care-free future–quite the opposite. Lottery winners, inheritors of fortunes, stock market gurus, and wise money managers have experienced disaster within their families and their personal lives because their future was based on the love of money rather than loving God and others. Whether you come from new money or old, whether you worked your tail off for money or it was handed to you, if you don't have love for others, your future will likely be a lonesome one. If you don't have love, you are like a noisy gong or clanging symbol (1 Corinthians 13:1).

Putting all your eggs in the money basket or some other basket, is never a good or wise decision for a future of contentment. You won't satisfy yourself or others. At the end of life, when there is no one to hold your hand or shed a tear for you, you may mourn your life as you lived it. That is a great embarrassment for many a person and would bring a blush until your eyelids close one last time.

So, put your trust in that Person, and as the old song says:
Put your hand in the hand of the man who stills the water;
Put your hand in the hand of the man who calmed the sea

Take a look at yourself and you can look at others differently
Put your hand in the hand of the man from Galilee. [JESUS]
When you do this, your future is secured for eternity.

Chapter Thirteen

# TEEN TALK

*"Out of the mouths of babies and infants, you have established strength..."*

Psalm 8:2

I t is one thing to voice personal comments of a senior citizen (a.k.a., the author) about the lack of civility in the populace of America, but it is another thing to survey the upcoming generations and listen to their take on the subject of civility. As an old man, I have little connection to teenagers or 20-year-olds. I do, however, have grandchildren in that age group. For the most part, they are super conservative, and probably somewhat biased in favor of civility and good manners. Nevertheless, I have asked for some feedback from the younger generations to get their views of civility in their America.

Below are the five questions that were asked of a random sampling of younger people, followed by their various responses.

1. Have you taken any courses on manners, civility, or politeness in school? (Kindergarten through High School)

2. How would you describe the vocabulary, mannerisms, and overall conduct of young people today?

3. Do you believe, in general, that people are rude to each other in our modern society?

4. If you think that good manners, conduct, and politeness need improving, how would you suggest doing it?

5. Who influences your behavior the most?

## Joshua, age 11

Joshua said that he had been taught manners in elementary school. He sees some people polite enough to hold doors for others – sometimes. Others say "please" and "thank you," but not too many. Most people he sees are stupid and rude. His suggestion to improve manners starts with parental training. His mother influences him the most.

## Bryce, age 13

Bryce was taught manners in elementary school. He said many teens use lots of curse words, especially the "F" word, and they don't care who hears it, even girls. His suggestion to improve conduct and civility is to introduce people to Jesus. His father influences him the most.

## Olivia, age 14

Olivia stated that she was not taught manners in school, but she did have some Bible classes in manners. Conduct and manners are slangish and lazy, and rudeness depends on the part of the country in which you live. Urban or suburban environments make a huge difference in manners. Her suggestion to improve civility is to return to the character of youth before the hippies, when morality took a beating and went down. Her worst influences come from TV and movies, where characters talk, act, and think in immoral ways.

## Marissa, age 24

Marissa was taught manners in elementary school; however, it was not extensive teaching, and there was no real follow-up from teachers in action or word. She emphasized that teen manners are almost non-existent because of the progressive culture that says young people are allowed to do what makes them feel in charge and what makes them feel good. She feels that people, in general, are rude to each other, and that there is no set program to improve mannerisms, conduct, or politeness, unless parents start teaching their children. Parents must teach that everyone is valuable, and it is important to be considerate of all. She stated: "Youth today are focused on themselves and do whatever makes them feel good."

Her opinion is that people are rude to each other and they are not trying to improve. She believes it is almost impossible to re-train adults to be kind and considerate. Values need to be demonstrated to children along with an explanation of why manners and civility are important. She encourages (or highly suggests) that people, especially youth, get rid of the egocentric mindset and put-on community fellowship and camaraderie.

Marissa's parents were her biggest influencers and she wants to be the influencer of her children so that they possess manners, civility, and character pleasing to all, and especially to God.

\*\*\*\*\*\*\*\*\*\*\*\*\*\*\*\*\*\*\*\*\*\*\*\*\*\*\*\*\*\*\*\*\*\*\*

Not only did I get some good information from youngsters, but in a Facebook survey, older Americans chimed in with their observations.

Different questions were asked of these adults:

1. Do you think blushing is still a part of American culture?

2. Do you blush?

3. What makes you blush, if you do?

4. Have you seen civility, decorum, and manners change over the years?

5. Are today's young people more or less polite, civil, kind, and helpful than when you were growing up?

## Male, age 35
He was never taught manners in school. His opinion is that manners, conduct, and civility have degraded greatly in his lifetime. In addition, he feels that vocabulary and good speech have degenerated into coarse talk and ignorant ramblings.

## Female, age 36
She doesn't think blushing is common today, but she does blush. It is usually when people talk about something naughty, or she is talking in front of a group. She feels young people are less civil and possess a "me first" attitude. People are in a self-focused mood today. It's all about "me."

## Female, age 45
She believes blushing does still exist, but not as a part of the younger culture. She blushes at bad language in front of her children and when someone purposely tries to embarrass her. People don't hold doors or use polite words. However, she sees that some

young people do show signs of goodness, civility, and kindness, but it is the few and far between.

## Female, age 63
She believes blushing is a very small part of our culture. She still blushes at coarse jokes. She has seen our culture change quite a bit over the years. Most teens are much less polite that when she was young.

## Female, age 65
She thinks blushing is rare in our culture today. She blushes less than when she was younger. Not as much shocks her now as it did in years past. It's not because she doesn't think it's wrong, but it has just become more common. Her disgust is more her reactions to bad language and clothing. After 21 years of teaching young teens, she is quick to mention that some of them are kind, polite, and sensitive young people. She thinks these teens still exist, but those young people who are not civil seem to be the focus of the media, the ones idolized by the public. Because we have been focused on the uncivil young people, it's hard to see those who are civil. "My generation was known for its rebellion and drug use, but I think the young generation now, as a whole, is less polite, kind, and helpful."

## Female, age 70
"Yes, I blush at depravity, lewdness, and immorality in our nation world, and church. However, I'm encouraged to know of youth and many young adults who are blushing also and who mourn over this condition of our nation and world. It seems most of the young generation is without manners, except for a few. We have been desensitized to sin through TV, media, and the new methods of education."

## Female, age 84

"I could write you a book on the changes in my lifetime. On everything and in every way. It is not the same. The culture accepts everything, every lifestyle! I can hardly believe some of the changes. Old people were respected. Wrong was wrong. People were not respected that are embraced now in our society. Nothing is frowned on now. I am an 84-year-old female and glad that I grew up when right was right and wrong was wrong."

\*\*\*\*\*\*\*\*\*\*\*\*\*\*\*\*\*\*\*\*\*\*\*\*\*\*\*\*\*\*

Finally, I asked two teenagers to write an essay on their thoughts regarding civility. Fourteen-year-old Chloe from Mobile, Alabama, and 15-year-old Will from Ocala, Florida, wrote with great insight and maturity.

## Here is Chloe's report:

In so many ways teenagers are much different now than they were a hundred, or even 50 years ago. In my opinion, our ancestors would be humiliated if they could see how young people talk and act in our modern world. Teenagers used to be taught to show others respect and kindness, especially to their elders. They would say 'please', and 'thank you' and they would say 'excuse me' when they were passing someone. If they saw someone who needed help with carrying their groceries or doing their yardwork, teens would drop what they were doing and go to help. Now, teens often brush past people without a second glance. Very few teenagers show genuine respect, kindness or modesty any more. In fact, we can just listen to the news to hear how young people are being bullied daily at schools and in neighborhoods. In my opinion, and I'm allowed to say this because I am one, many young people are rude and lazy. I have often observed the expectations of children and teenagers to be highest priority for parents. I know many kids my age, and younger, who expect a phone with all the latest apps and accessories. It isn't a matter of earning a phone or a car, it is that children feel it is their right to have the items, and the duty of parents to provide them.

Throughout my reading and study of history, I have learned that past generations of girls wore clothes long enough to cover themselves for modesty. Many girls today are wearing their clothes shorter and shorter. They don't care how immodest their clothes are, especially their bathing suits and shorts. I am embarrassed for them. I blush when I see their lack of concern for modesty and safety. Some people may not agree with my opinion, but I feel that when girls expose their bodies in public or on the computer, they are recklessly stirring up feelings and desires in boys and men which contribute to the potential for rapes, trafficking and abuse. The people who commit such crimes are solely responsible and accountable for their actions, and they should be punished. At the same time, women and girls need to be responsible for their lifestyle choices.

It is not even uncommon to see girls wearing short, strapless, form-fitting dresses to church. It used to be normal for girls and boys to wear their best clothing. Now, young people seem to choose the most comfortable clothing without respect for the worship of God. In my church, I have seen girls come in with outfits that barely cover them from armpits to behinds. My sister and I have to look away because we are embarrassed at what is being revealed. These girls can't even sit down comfortably because of the shortness or tightness of their clothing. I'm embarrassed to have my dad and brothers see what is right in front of them when we are supposed to be worshipping God.

Boys and girls used to conduct themselves with dignity and civility, and they were careful to avoid foul language. They used to be taught to give up their seats to their elders in buses or waiting rooms. Now, if teenagers don't get what they want, when they want it, they spew off using ugly words. They don't care if someone is without a seat; they just continue doing their own thing, ignoring whoever is without a seat. I have read about how teens and children used to act and speak to people. I have also seen it in TV shows, and I believe that teens today are sorely lacking in manners and etiquette. Male teens used to hold doors open for people, they used to be very respectful to women and girls. Men used to be careful about cursing in front of women; now, men and women both curse regularly.

Well-mannered teens used to care about what they read or viewed on a regular basis; they avoided people who practiced magic and who drank. Now, teens watch vampire shows, horror movies, or read books about magic such as *Harry Potter*. They sneak alcohol and pot at school and at home. I realize that throughout the centuries, kids did dumb things. However, it seems that the code of civility and right/wrong standards has disappeared. The Bible verse, "Everyone did what was right in his own eyes" seems very appropriate to today's world, just as it was in ancient days. (Judges 17:6)

According to first hand sources, children and teens kept quiet when sitting with adults to show respect and not to burst out talking and interrupt a conversation. Children were to be seen and not heard as a sign of respect; they were to be in the background. Children played outside in the sunshine, and when they were old enough, they went to work, whether it was in the fields or in town. Teens did a good days work every day. Teens would work for hours, eat a good meal, and go to bed tired. On top of that, they went to school and made good grades. Kids used to try their very best to make good grades because if they did, they could go to college and do something with their lives. College was a privilege that had to be earned, something that teens now take for granted.

In the past few years, world-wide morality has gone down the drain. Politics play a large part in that because many politicians don't care how many people they crush or hurt as long as they get the power; infinite power. Fewer and fewer teens know right from wrong anymore because adults have so many twisted and screwed up opinions you can't tell who's got the correct definition. Because morality has gone down, fewer people are honest anymore. They choose to cover up their plans and deceive other people to get everything they want while the people they are taking things away from have to make daily sacrifices to provide for their families, which is something these people will never understand, or have to go through.

After thinking through this chapter, maybe it isn't so much that teens are worse now than ever. Maybe it is that we are experiencing a recurring downward shift in morality due to our ever-changing society.

## The following is Will's report:

My report is not exactly a survey report but an opinion report on how I see society today and especially young people in the light of civility, mannerisms, and politeness.

Civility is defined by Merriam-Webster dictionary as: "Civilized conduct, especially as it relates to courtesy, politeness, and manners." It only takes a quick observation of our society to realize that both civility and manners are becoming less and less noticeable. There are probably a number of reasons why this has happened. I want to take this opportunity to share some observations from my life that I believe have contributed to this.

I believe that the three most important places of learning for civility and manners are the home, the church and school. I want to begin with school. I have never been taught any courses that were specifically about civility or manners. There were certain teachers that made a point to teach the students the importance of manners, but that was not part of their lesson plan. As far as I know, there are no classes or curriculums that are designed to teach students about manners. I understand they use to be taught years ago throughout the elementary school years.

It has been my experience that the home and church provide the most significant influences for a student in regard to training in civility. This may not be true for everyone, because not everyone attends church and there are many different home environments. For me, my parents and close Christian mentors have been the greatest influence for my behavior and manners. This is a good thing when you come from a stable, positive home, but that is not true for everyone.

I believe that this is one of the main reasons that people are rude towards one another. When their home or personal life is not the greatest, they take out their anger and frustration on other people. I also think teenagers want to be popular and want to act all big, bad, and tough. Sometimes this causes them to be rude to someone because they think it will help them fit in with their peers. Overall, I do not believe that students are rude because they like being rude. I just don't think that they realize how bad their language or conduct is towards other people.

The vocabulary used by a lot of young people today is obscene. I think that is mostly due to the culture around them. Many students are told from a young age that it is OK to curse and use foul language. Also, that is the type of language they hear all the time. After a while, it ends up becoming natural to you. As far as the manners used today, I believe they are also a result of how someone was brought up. I think that the role models and leaders in a person's life will definitely influence how polite they are. This could be a teacher, coach, parent, grandparent, professor, older sibling or any combination. I have found that people who were taught manners at a very young age by their parents and other leaders continue to use those good manners today.

The conduct of teenagers really isn't great either. In my experience, the culture teaches students that it is cool to do drugs and drink alcohol and have sex before marriage. When society says it is OK to do something and everyone around you is giving in to these practices of bad conduct that makes it very difficult to act differently. This is why so many people have bad conduct no matter how they were brought up, because it is difficult for them to go against the grain. Unfortunately, if it is that hard for people who were brought up well and taught proper manners and conduct, then it becomes exponentially harder for young people who have been raised in a more negative environment to stand firm. Peer pressure is a powerful adversary.

Even though practicing civility, manners and good conduct is a challenge in this society, I do believe there are ways for us to improve. I think it definitely begins in the home with parents, but I also believe there is something that can be done on a more widespread level. I would suggest having teachers teach curriculum and classes on civility and manners at the elementary level. They need to take the time to teach the kids to have manners. If there is a way to send homework home for the students to practice with their families, then that might influence the home as well. Studies show that on average it takes about 66 days for something to become automatic. So, if children are taught manners throughout the elementary level then that might help. It will definitely be hard to do anything without changing the culture first, but that is something not just one person can do. That is something that only a group of people who are willing to stand up for what they believe in can do.

My name is Will and I pray that anyone, who has the power and reads this report, will use his/her power to insist that children in our public schools get some instructions in manners and deportment.

******************************

These reports from two teenagers reflect personal opinions. If anyone with an open mind and honest character looks around at the moral status of our kids today, it is evident there has been a decline in manners in the last few years that borders on an epidemic of moral decay. Only by a concentrated effort on the part of concerned parents, teachers, preachers, or Christian counselors will the moral foundation of the nation be turned around for the better.

Chapter Fourteen

# CHURCHES AND OVERSEERS

*"Fine speech is not becoming to a fool; still less is false speech to a prince."*

Proverbs 17:7

*"Every way of a man is right to his own eyes, but the LORD weighs the heart."*

Proverbs 21:2

*"But I have this against you, that you have abandoned the love you had at first."*

Revelation 2:4

It may be stretching the theme of this book when it comes to blushing in regards to church and overseers.

By "church," I am referring to the members, and the "overseers" as the leaders of the flock. Blushing comes from many different feelings, ranging from embarrassment, to shame, to disgrace, to failure. Do churches and overseers take on any of these traits?

Absolutely. But they also excel in the ministry of God's Holy Word, and they touch lives for Jesus all around the world.

It is with great care that I would criticize any church or overseer. I do believe we who sit in the pews need to be observant, similar to the Bereans of Acts 17:11. They examined the scriptures "daily to see if these things were so" as Paul and Silas preached to them. Christians have a responsibility to follow the model of the Bereans to evaluate what our preachers say, the religious books we read, and the traditions or rituals we may be asked to follow.

Psalm 1 shows us the way of the Righteous and the way of the Wicked. There is a distinction between one who listens to ungodly (worldly) counsel and one who meditates on God's Word. The person "who walks not in the counsel of the wicked, nor stands in the way of sinners, nor sits in the seats of scoffers" will be blessed, and "his delight is in the law of the LORD, and on his law he meditates day and night." (Psalm 1:1-2)

Paul's ministry to the church was "to make the Word of God fully known...Christ in you, the hope of glory [to] present everyone mature in Christ" (Col. 1:25-28). We are to follow preachers who take on this mindset and churches who adhere to these instructions with doctrinal statements and faithful action. It is the believer's responsibility to "Beware lest any man spoil you through philosophy and vain deceit, after the tradition of man, after the rudiments of the world, and not after Christ" (Col. 2:8 KJV).

In Ezekiel 33, God refers to the prophet as a watchman, or sentry, observing the dangers of a coming enemy. Normally, this would be an external physical enemy, but here he is to be a watchman for the Israelites in spiritual matters. The enemy seeking to destroy the people was their own sinful ways and disregard for God's Word. I am convinced that the task of every born-again believer in Jesus Christ is to be a watchman.

God cautions Ezekiel that if he does not sound the trumpet and warn the people of false teachers or false doctrines, he will be guilty and their blood will be on his head. Conversely, if he warns them and they don't repent, their blood is on their own heads.

Be warned about listening to ungodly advice. Are you listening to the counsel of celebrities, politicians, immature believers, or unbelievers? Is the church infatuated with Oprah, Ellen, or Joel? Every word you hear should be measured against Scripture.

Our nation is pluralistic, supporting churches of many faiths and denominations. Each has its doctrinal foundation based on the guiding beliefs of its members and leaders. In a 2017 Gallup poll, 48.5% of Americans claimed to be Protestant or other Christian, 22.7% Catholic, 1.8% Mormon, 2.1% Jewish, 0.8% Muslim, 2.9% other religions, and 21.3% gave no religious identity (Newport). It must be understood that not all religions in our country use the Holy Bible as their faith book upon which to establish their religious beliefs. For evangelical followers of Jesus Christ, the Holy Bible, with its inspiration and inerrancy, is the guiding light by which they are encouraged to live.

While critics like to complain about the failure of churches and overseers, believers should agree that it is of paramount importance to lift up in prayer to God these churches, organizations, missionaries, and dedicated laity who give their all to spread the Good News across the world. We shall proclaim them faithful followers of Christ in this chapter.

Before evaluating churches and overseers, it may be worthwhile to define what the church really is. Recently, I read an article by Marv Rosenthal from *Zion's Fire* magazine entitled, "Defining the Church." Here is my summation of his descriptions of the church:

The church, properly understood, is not a building. It is a called-out assembly from every tongue, kindred, or tribe.

The church, properly understood, is not an organization, it is a living organism; the Head being Jesus Christ. [Ephesians 4:15]

The church, properly understood, is not a denomination, it is a group of individuals who have faith in Jesus Christ.

The church, properly understood, cannot be entered by natural birth, inheritance, lifestyle, religious affiliation, baptism, or purchase. It is entered by Spiritual birth.

The church, properly understood, should always strive for unity in the body, but not at the sacrifice of biblical truth. [Philippians 1:15-18]

The church, properly understood, is not without experience or emotion, but is not guided by either. It is guided by God's Holy Word.

The church, properly understood, is not only intangible and universal, it is also physical and local.

The church, properly understood, is not synonymous with Christendom, those who *profess* Jesus but do not *possess* Him. The church is composed of *possessors* of the new nature of Christ and indwelt by the Holy Spirit. "And then will I declare to them, 'I never knew you;' depart from me, you workers of lawlessness.'" (Matthew 7:23)

The church, properly understood, is not a social club, political platform, business transaction facility, or place for self-centered achievements. It is a place where biblical doctrine is taught, ordinances are observed, discipline administered, and where saints gather in worship of Jesus Christ. "Bear one another's burdens, and so fulfill the law of Christ." (Galatians 6:2)

The church, properly understood, is established for one overriding purpose – to glorify God by being a reflection to humanity of what God is like, through worship, through edification and evangelizing the lost.

## CHURCHES

Acts 2:42-47 describes the function of the body of believers within the church. Under the Lordship of Christ:

> ...they devoted themselves to the apostle's teaching [discipleship] and the fellowship, to the breaking of bread and the prayers. And awe came upon every soul, and many wonders and signs were being done through the apostles. And all who believed were together and had all things in common. And they were selling their possessions and belongings and distributing the proceeds to all, as any had need [stewardship]. And day by day, attending the temple together and breaking bread in their homes [worship], they received their food with glad and generous hearts, praising God and having favor with all the people. And the Lord added to their number day by day those who were being saved.

Many churches today are struggling. The pandemic of 2020 shut down churches and limited fellowship. Some churches are able to use Zoom, Skype, or other internet sources to communicate, but those who are without computers or iPhones have no chance of connecting with brothers and sisters in Christ. Even those with these electronic marvels are out of touch with their religious leaders and friends. It is a trying time for the moral and spiritual backbone of our nation – the church.

Nevertheless, churches of America are strong and resilient even in these struggling times. Some do fail and close their doors, but many others are true to the Gospel and Jesus' directive as stated in Matthew 28:19-20: "Go ...Baptize ...Teach." Missionaries reach out to the whole world, taking the Good News to those who have never heard of a man called Jesus and how He can change their lives for eternity.

As we look at churches and overseers, it's very easy to key in on the negative aspects of both. It is easy to be a watchman and sound a warning of approaching spiritual danger. It is easy, but it isn't fair because there are still churches and overseers doing a thankless task of spreading the Word under organized resistance from man and spirits.

For the next few pages, we will look at the following activities within our churches and see where we can be useful in improving them, encouraging the participants, and yes, sounding the trumpet on those who have failed to teach the truth of the Gospel. We will look at:

- Money/Giving
- Attendance
- Volunteers
- Edification (Training – making disciples)

## Money/Giving

Many professing Christians are selfish. They do not obey the directive: "Bring the full tithe into the storehouse, that there may be food in my house. And thereby put me to the test, says the LORD of hosts, if I will not open the windows of heaven for you and pour down for you a blessing until there is no more need." (Malachi 3:10)

This is an awesome promise from God. The question is, Why don't Christians obey?

As 2020 draws to a close, churches and ministry organizations tell us that giving into the storehouses of God has declined. It is a blessing of God that some churches have faithful members who have continued to give, such as the obedient ones in my church. Praise God!!

All people have bills to pay. Bills that provide for our physical well-being. Churches also have financial responsibilities, such as salaries, facility upkeep, local and world-wide mission support, benevolent actions, training, equipment, and a host of other expenditures. What about our spiritual well-being? In all honesty, our spiritual well-being is infinitely more important than our physical. We need to do what we can to keep our entire life pleasing to God. This includes giving. We want our churches and overseers to function at their maximum. They can only do this when their physical needs are met by faithful, giving members.

Giving should be a worshipful experience. One church that I previously attended had a unique way of taking their tithes and offerings. They literally obeyed 2 Corinthians 9:6-7, "…whoever sows sparingly will also reap sparingly, and whoever sows bountifully will also reap bountifully. Each one must give as he has decided in his heart, not reluctantly or under compulsion, for God loves a cheerful giver." Cheerful is translated from the Greek word "hilarom," from which we get our word "hilarious." That was the scene at this church when the offering plates were passed. The congregation would rise with a shout of acclamation, laughter, and applause. It was an exhilarating experience, a delightful experience, and a serious worshipful experience that many churches have never enjoyed.

Have you noticed that many churches are marketing the ease of online giving? Obviously, with our national stay-at-home mandates, church members have not been able to give during worship services. For some, online tithing began long before the coronavirus-mandated cessation of church services. However, since the pandemic started, more and more pastors and staff are urging members to give online because it is easier, more convenient, and you "don't even have to think about it because the money can be automatically deducted from your bank account and sent to your church." Even with churches opening back up, giving online is promoted as *the* way to give. Every week we hear how we can make our lives simpler and less stressful by giving online. Since when is giving supposed to be easy and convenient? The truth is, giving should be a worshipful experience, and giving online removes any semblance of worship.

In 2 Samuel 24:24, King David was told to build an altar on the threshing floor of Araunah the Jebusite. Araunah freely offered the floor, oxen, wood, and men to help David. David's response should stir our hearts when it comes to giving to the Lord. He said, "I will not offer burnt offerings to the LORD my God that cost me nothing."

The poor widow's story is told in Mark 12:41-44. She contributed two small coins to the offering box; all that she had. She gave with reverence, sacrificially, and with a heart of worship. In contrast, others gave from their abundance. They gave carelessly, pridefully, and with no heart-worship involved. It wasn't easy or convenient for the widow, yet Jesus praised her for her sacrifice, obedience, and worship.

It is heartbreaking to hear the Sunday morning message prefaced with all the convenient ways to give money to the church: through an app on your phone, through texting, and through automatic bank payments. Where is the reverence? Where is the respect and remembrance of our Christian history of sacrifice and selflessness? If giving is a part of worship, why are we being encouraged to find the easiest way to send money to the church?

We ought to be ashamed for building bigger barns (Luke 12:18). Why do we build huge church buildings? Why do we add gyms, softball fields, and vast parking lots to our church campuses? Are these things for the glory of Christ or for entertainment of the saints? Why don't we take the millions of dollars spent for building projects and fund missionaries instead? Why do we go into debt for bigger and better worship centers? Why don't we take this money and use it for scholarships for young people in our churches who feel called to ministry and missions? What if the church paid for college or seminary students' education so they would not be strapped with debt; debt which may keep them from going to the mission field? Why do we have no problem with spending thousands of dollars for a Disney vacation, yet dropping a ten dollar bill into the offering plate feels like we are sacrificing?

This is a time for many to be ashamed and blush and give with more reverence.

## Attendance

Not accounting for stay-at-home orders during the pandemic of 2020, church attendance is dwindling. Many overseers feel that the church needs to supply entertainment to get people to attend. Church members and visitors like to attend when some fabulous entertainment is presented. In past years, people went to church for social activities – that was the primary meeting place. The church provided Bible study, prayer, and ministry to all attendees. Where are church members today? At the beach, Disney, on their boats or RVs, shopping, at work, with travel sports teams, or just chilling out.

Kent Shaffer writes about one church's evaluation of fun events. They discovered that "while they're [fun events] great at getting people to attend church and say they're Christians that the unfortunate majority of their congregation is in a state of arrested spiritual development. They discovered that their approach was great at Christian baby-making, but they couldn't disciple them past being bottle fed by the pulpit and into learning to spiritually feed themselves and abide in Christ like John 15 expresses."

So, when does church attendance grow? I know it grows in times of disasters. It grows when a celebrity is filling the pulpit. It grows when comedians or entertainers are performing. Numbers rise at Christmas and Easter. People come to watch their children or grandchildren sing and act. I have seen plenty of new faces at concerts, promotional events, and advertised celebrations.

Attendance numbers at church used to grow for the right reasons. Vacation Bible Schools boost attendance with children who learn from Bible stories, displays, art work, and fellowship, and they pass the gospel message on to interested parents or guardians about what they learned. That's a win-win situation for young and old. There were times when revivals filled the pews with people who wanted to learn the Word of the Lord. Evangelists Dwight L. Moody, Billy Sunday, George Whitefield, Charles Finney, John and Charles Wesley, Jonathan Edwards, and one of the greatest evangelists of modern times, Billy Graham, could really pack the pews and stadiums. When those men preached, churches, venues, ball-parks, and tents were filled with people from all walks of life coming to hear a good old Gospel sermon. They were not entertained. They were challenged, convicted, edified, and enlightened about their spiritual condition and how, "… to present your bodies as a living sacrifice, holy and acceptable to God, which is your spiritual worship." (Romans 12:1)

All these activities are bringing people into the church. The next question is, How do we get them to stay and commit to the Lord's service? The answer is expressed in John 13:34-35 when Jesus says, "A new commandment I give to you, that you love one another: just as I have loved you, you also are to love one another. By this all people will know that you are my disciples, if you have love for one another." We can show love in a number of ways to those newcomers who have come in from out of the cold, hard world to find the "...peace of God, which surpasses all understanding..." (Phil. 4:7)

The following is a list of things every church member can do to turn an estranged visitor into a dedicated disciple and productive member of the fellowship:

- Listen: Listen to the needs of the potential member.
- Gentle touch: Reach out to them.
- Pick up the phone and give them a call after their visit.
- Make meals: Take them a meal or take them out to dinner.
- Put air in their tires: Start a Car Care Day for widows/widowers, single ladies, etc.
- Compliments mean a lot: Praise them for something.
- Send a card: Start a card care ministry.
- Take them to Bible study: Take them, don't just invite them.
- Come alongside: Help them understand the Bible; introduce them to Biblical commentaries.

It is with sadness that I believe cults do a better job of discipling than Christians do. They apply all the above tasks, excluding Bible truths, to grasp and hold potential converts to their way of life. They isolate, educate, demand obedience, demonstrate unity, and brainwash their selected new followers with a powerful zeal for their cause. Of course, their doctrine and beliefs are diametrically opposed to making disciples through love, compassion, and the truth of the Bible as Christians believe.

## Volunteers

A startling fact within churches is that 20% of the flock does most of the work. The old axiom, "Good help is hard to find," is especially true in the church. However, there is another startling fact. The Holy Spirit imparts spiritual gifts to <u>ALL</u> born-again

Christians so that every part of the church's ministry is covered. The difficulty is helping each member find his or her spiritual gift and then encouraging each one to use it.

For the past few months in our Wednesday evening Bible class, we've been studying "The Wonders, Ways, and Workings of the Holy Spirit." One subject was the motivational gifts given to each born-again person, to be used for the furtherance of God's Kingdom. In Romans 12:6-8, Paul compares the gifts as being similar to the parts of the body. It takes many parts of the human body to keep it functioning properly. Likewise, it takes Christians with various gifts to keep the church functioning efficiently. Christians can discover their spiritual gifts by taking simple online tests. God gives us these talents and desires us to use them for His Glory.

Churches are pleading for volunteers to help in Sunday School, Vacation Bible School, widows/widowers visits, food preparation and delivery, prison ministry, Good News Club in local schools, teaching English as a Second Language (ESL), disaster relief, assisted-living Bible studies, home visitation, and most importantly-reaching the lost. There are many ways to serve God in the church and in the community. The theme of a Christian's life is not to be "saved and sit," but to be "saved and serve." Too many Christians are sitting, and too few are serving. Those that are sitting ought to be embarrassed by their lack of action and get busy serving the Lord while utilizing the talents given by the Holy Spirit.

There is a caution that must be observed when assigning members to a position in the church. Sometimes there is a tendency to just throw a body at the open position. That is like the proverbial fitting of a square peg into a round hole. The member's spiritual gift(s) should be discovered through a spiritual gifts test, and then prayerfully matched to a place of service. We (the church) should be intentional about training members, especially those assigned to leadership roles. Training should start with children who display leadership qualities and love to follow Christian mentors.

## Edification

Edification refers to the moral or intellectual instruction of a person. This is part of the function of the church and its leaders – to build up the flock unto good works. (Hebrews 10:24-25) Paul tells Timothy, and us, that Scripture comes from God to teach us, correct us, and equip us to do God's will. It is profitable for salvation, sanctification, and Christian growth. (2 Timothy 3:15-17) The Scriptures provide a road map to Heaven, as well as a road map to right living here on earth.

When a person is saved, the making of a disciple of Jesus begins. Churches used to post on their nickels – and – noses boards their baptisms, tithing, and attendance numbers. How many Christians today rejoice at the number of sold-out-to-Jesus disciples in their midst? How does the church evaluate whether a disciple has been made?

Making disciples and training people is not an easy task. We have many professing believers on our membership rolls who fit this description by Paul:

> You have been Christians a long time now, and you ought to be teaching others, but instead you have dropped back to the place where you need someone to teach you all over again the very first principles in God's Word. You are like babies who can drink only milk, not old enough for solid food. And when a person is still living on milk it shows he isn't very far along in the Christian life, and doesn't know much about the difference between right

and wrong. He is still a baby Christian! (Hebrews 5:12-13 TLB)

Addressing maturing Christians, Paul writes: "Work hard so God can say to you, 'Well done.' Be a good workman, one who does not need to be ashamed when God examines your work. Know what his Word says and means." (2 Timothy 2:15 TLB). Here is clearly stated the effort of growing in the knowledge of God by studying the Word of God. We need trained and equipped overseers to come alongside and disciple us in the truth.

This underscores our need to find a Bible-believing, mission-minded, soul-winning local church where we can sit under the leadership of men and women committed to the edification of the saints. There are many self-help books and programs available to sharpen our understanding of the Scriptures so that we may be equipped to present the plan of salvation clearly and boldly. The Romans Road, Evangelism Explosion, The Faith Road, and many other methods of sharing the Gospel are widely used and faithfully followed. The best program that I have found for helping others to grow as a Christian and to witness to others is the Teacher Training Course(TCE1) from Child Evangelism Fellowship (CEF) – the Good News Club. This course can be reviewed at CEF.com. It is taught by certified teachers to help believers minister to others, especially children; get off the spiritual milk of immaturity and partake of the meat of the Scriptures. It will change your life, the life of your church, and most certainly, the lives of all who hear.

We see from Scripture that God built His church for three primary reasons:

**Reason #1: To be a fellowship of baptized believers in Christ, bonded together to carry the Good News to all mankind (Matthew 28:19-20)**

In Matthew 28:19-20, Jesus gives His church its marching orders: "Therefore go and make disciples of all nations, baptizing them in the name of the Father and of the Son and of the Holy Spirit, and teaching them to obey everything I have commanded you." (KJV) We are to evangelize locally and worldwide.

Since the early church, missionaries have left home, family, and friends to take the Gospel to all the world. They are giving their lives so others will be saved. We observe individuals and mission organizations busy translating the Bible into local languages and dialects so people can hear and read the Word of the Lord in their own language. When trained, they can teach the message of hope to others of their native tongue. We must faithfully support missions at home and abroad so the truth of God's Word will reach people of "every tribe and language and people and nation" who will, one day, stand before the throne and worship the Lamb (Revelation 5:9; 7:9).

I am proud of the CEF organization and their Good News Clubs for children. In 2018 more than 25,000,000 children were involved in Clubs around the world. They sang, played, listened to Bible stories, memorized Bible verses, and heard about Jesus and the plan of salvation. Thousands gave their lives to the Lord. CEF has followed Jesus' instructions to go into the world, and the Word is bearing fruit.

**Reason #2: To be a fellowship of baptized believers in Christ, bonded together for mutual encouragement, protection, sustenance, edification, training, and love, according to God's Holy Word, and under the direction of the Holy Spirit (Hebrews 10:24-25; Colossians 13:12-17)**

Where can you go when you are hurting emotionally, physically, or spiritually? Who can you call when you are in despair? How can you be trained to do good? Where will you find acceptance and love beyond compare? These are questions that should be answered within the bonds of a fellowship of baptized believers in Christ – His holy church.

Read the end of Hebrews 10 to see how the writer encouraged believers to meet together for love and good works, as a demonstration of their faith in Christ Jesus. Paul and Timothy tell us to put on, or clothe, ourselves with:

1. compassion
2. kindness
3. humility
4. meekness
5. patience
6. forbearance
7. forgiveness
8. love
9. peace
10. thankfulness
11. wisdom

In the past, the church was a place of learning and support. The teachings of the church were carried over into school classrooms. Everything in the community revolved around the church and its biblical principles. Times have changed, and not for the better. Many believers have lost sight of their mandate to love one another; in particular, to love the body of believers.

The church is not a building. The church is a group of people. We need each other. We must not be lone-ranger Christians. All over our land people are lonely. Widows, widowers, single-parents, orphans, neglected children, homeless, and the poor fill the houses and line the streets of our neighborhoods. We so often overlook the needy all around us. They would cherish attention and assistance from people who claim to care. Many churches do so little to help. We are too busy. We are spread too thin. We have our own issues to deal with. We don't know what to do. As a result of our inaction, people suffocate in their loneliness and isolation.

Some beacons of hope burn brightly in our communities: Christian-sponsored children's homes; boys and girls ranches; homes for unwed mothers, similar to John Hagee's Sanctuary of Hope in San Antonio; widow's ministries; and many other excellent works. The need is great. All churches, boasting of a fellowship of baptized believers, must dedicate their services and resources to the needy, not only inside their fellowship, but also in the outer community.

While the global pandemic rages on, isolated people are struggling, not knowing when normal life will return. Anxiety, stress, depression, fear, loneliness, anger, and suicides are some of the physical and psychological effects of this virus that may last a long time. People are hungry for fellowship with others. The universal Church should be rushing to meet the needs of a strained world.

**Reason #3: To be a fellowship of baptized believers in Christ, bonded together to be presented to Him as a glorious church, having no spot or wrinkle, but holy and without blemish at His coming (Ephesians 5:27)**

What a beautiful picture it is that the church is called the Bride of Christ (referenced in Ephesians 5 and Revelation 19:7). Paul compared the union of husband and wife with that of Jesus and the church. The church (followers of Jesus) will be presented to Jesus in splendor.

The church of Jesus Christ is a living organism with many parts. Some have fallen away. (Matthew 24:10-11) Some have lost their first love (Revelation 2) and replaced it with worldly pleasures, programs, and societal accoutrements in attempts to entertain the flock and the world around them, "the love of many will grow cold" (Matthew 24:12). Simon Peter writes of the return of the Lord Jesus Christ. He explains that in the last days scoffers will come, following their own desires. Peter reminds believers that the Lord will fulfill His promises, tarrying, not wanting anyone to perish. The return of Jesus will come suddenly. We should be ready, living lives of holiness and godliness. Jesus' followers are to "be diligent to be found by him without spot or blemish, and at peace" (2 Peter 3:14). When we follow Jesus, we will be joined with Him on that grand reunion day in the clouds (1 Thessalonians 4:13-18).

## OVERSEERS

While I am not a pastor, or priest (overseer), and certainly not a prophet, I am an observer. Amos, in the Old Testament, said he was not a prophet, but he was appointed by God. He observed the priests of his time and offered positive advice for them to follow God's directives. They did not, and exile occurred for God's children.

As followers and observers of our spiritual overseers, we have opportunities to notice character traits and moral behavior. However, we are warned to "touch not my anointed ones, do my prophets no harm!"

> (Psalm 105:15) Therefore, I will not touch, I will not condemn, I will not accuse God's anointed.

Permit me to make some observations.

Pastors are under immense pressure from congregations and society at large. They are held under a microscope concerning their moral character. Reports abound of church leaders caught up in divorce or sexual scandals. From these things come a very clear understanding that overseers are persons who can and do sin. They are human.

In the early church of Acts 6, some were complaining that the needs of the widows were being overlooked. The overseers said, "It is not right that we should give up preaching the word of God to serve tables" (Acts 6:2). So the church chose godly men to serve the members. The overseers responded, "But we will devote ourselves to prayer and to the ministry of the word" (Acts 6:4). Paul gives to Timothy the qualifications for overseers:

> The saying is trustworthy: If anyone aspires to the office of overseer, he desires a noble task. Therefore an overseer must be above reproach, the husband of one wife, sober-minded, self-controlled, respectable, hospitable, able to teach, not a drunkard, not violent but gentle, not quarrelsome, not a love of money. He must manage his own household well, with all dignity keeping his children submissive, for if someone does not know how to manage his own household, how will he care for God's church? He must not be a recent convert, or he may become puffed up with conceit and fall into the condemnation of the devil. Moreover, he must be well thought of by outsiders, so that he may not fall into disgrace, into a snare of the devil. (1 Timothy 3:1-7)

Paul explains in his letter to Titus the qualifications of the elders (overseers) of the church:

> For an overseer, as God's steward, must be above reproach. He must not be arrogant or

quick-tempered or a drunkard or violent or greedy for gain; but hospitable, a lover of good, self-controlled, upright, holy, and disciplined. He must hold firm to the trustworthy word as taught, so that he may be able to give instruction in sound doctrine and also to rebuke those who contradict it. (Titus 1:7-9)

Pastors' duties are never done. They are called on 24 hours a day to minister to the flock. According to the Scriptures the pastor's main duty is to preach the Word and pray. Many present-day congregations expect the pastor to counsel, encourage, plan, perform weddings, conduct ordinances, reach the lost, execute disciplinary actions, mend broken spirits, and other duties as requested or assigned. They are to be men of all seasons.

It is every believer's duty to call out unrepentant men of God and false teachers. Second Timothy 4:3-4 reads: "For the time is coming when people will not endure sound teaching, but having itching ears they will accumulate for themselves teachers to suit their own passions, and will turn away from listening to the truth and wander off into myths." Today, false teachers and preachers abound in our society. We observe mega-churches that proliferate on "feel good" sermons. The people are not taught the Word of God. If an overseer is not preaching and practicing the words of our Holy Bible, we should avoid their leadership. "For there are many who are insubordinate, empty talkers and deceivers…Therefore rebuke them sharply, that they may be sound in the faith…They profess to know God, but they deny him by their works. They are detestable, disobedient, unfit for any good work" (Titus 1:10-16).

One prerequisite for being a watchman over any spiritual leader is to be a true believer in God, who is prayed up, confessed up, looking up, and living an obedient life. We must not call others sinful, wretched, unscrupulous, false teachers, depraved, and hell-bent when we may be full of the same moral depravity.

I mustn't leave this chapter without sharing another example of concern for the actions of overseers. At two large churches in a certain city of the United States, the pastors preached a series of sermons on super-heroes and Hollywood movies. I'm reasonably sure that spiritual application can be made about most any topic, but really? Hollywood super-hero movies? Why, oh why, is a pastor preaching about imaginary super heroes? Is this to entice the lost to come to church?

How do we act as a godly watchman to our spiritual leaders so that we are not judging, but led by God to ask our overseers to live in righteousness? When our overseers tickle the ears of the congregation instead of preaching Truth, we must stand firm in the Word of God.

# Chapter Fifteen

# PARENTAL GUIDANCE AND INVOLVEMENT

*"Train up a child in the way he should go; even when he is old he will not depart from it."*

Proverbs 22:6

The *National Fatherhood Initiative* tells us that there is a fatherhood absence crisis in America. "There is a 'father factor' in nearly all of the societal ills facing America today." Children with no father in the home are:

- 47% more likely to live in poverty
- 7 times more likely to become pregnant as a teen
- more likely to have behavioral problems
- more likely to face abuse and neglect
- more likely to abuse drugs and alcohol
- more likely to go to prison
- 2 times more likely to suffer obesity
- more likely to commit crime
- 2 times more likely to drop out of high school
- more likely to have depression

- more likely to be an absent dad themselves, or have children with an absent dad
- 4 times more likely to die within the first 28 days of their life
- 279% more likely to carry guns and deal drugs
- more likely to engage in delinquency ("The Proof Is In")

Gretchen Livingston points out that the percentage of U.S. children living with an unmarried parent jumped from 13% to 32% from 1968 – 2017. In fact, 7% of Asian children had a solo mother, 13% of White, 23% of Hispanic, and a staggering 47% of Black children, as of 2017, lived in a fatherless home.

How can young boys learn to be men when there is no father to train them?

How can young girls learn what to expect in future relationships without a father to model proper attributes?

So much regarding the turning around of our society depends upon parents, especially fathers. Home is the training ground. If parents fail to model and teach positive values, children will experience a deficit in moral standards. Parenting is a daunting task, and single-parent families are extremely vulnerable.

Proverbs 22:6, our beginning scripture in this chapter, is pertinent and important to parental involvement. This directive involves early childhood training. Some believe that learning and understanding occurs even in the womb. For this reason, parents play certain styles of music, recordings of different languages, or simply sing and talk to their child before birth. The most important training of children is conducted in the home by a dad and mom committed to each other and to the God of creation.

I have heard objections to Proverbs 22:6 from discouraged and disillusioned parents, mourning the fact that even though they raised their child right, that child rebelled against family, home, and religion. Keep in mind that the Proverbs are not promises from God. They are godly observations from the writers. If verse 6 were a promise, then it would seem to guarantee that the children of all believers would live to a ripe and blessed old age ("... even when he is old..."). This is not the case.

Children typically follow the patterns of their parents. Parents who drink or use drugs influence their children to do the same. Children of abusive or racist parents often duplicate those same destructive traits. When a parent is absent (physically or emotionally), children are more susceptible to less-than-desirable influences. At the same time, parents who teach and model honesty, integrity, kindness, generosity, compassion, and love will often reap the reward of children who practice these same attributes. However, if parents instruct in a biblical manner and act in a non-biblical manner, it is not surprising that grown children model their actions and not their words. Children are smart. When they observe hypocrisy, they take note of it. Ezekiel 18 indicates that righteous parents can have wicked children. Samuel was an example of a righteous man who had wicked sons. (1 Samuel 8:1-3)

The counsel from Proverbs 22:6 is that parents are to train their children to follow the ways of the Lord. Training includes more than mere words. Here is the idea, eloquently put into rhyme by Edgar Guest:

## Sermons We See

I'd rather see a sermon than hear one any day;
I'd rather one should walk with me than merely tell the way.
The eye's a better pupil and more willing than the ear,
Fine counsel is confusing, but example's always clear;
And the best of all the preachers
are the men who live their creeds,
For to see good put in action is what everybody needs.

I soon can learn to do it if you'll let me see it done;
I can watch your hands in action,
but your tongue too fast may run.
And the lecture you deliver may be very wise and true,
But I'd rather get my lessons by observing what you do;
For I might misunderstand you
and the high advise [sic] you give,
But there's no misunderstanding how you act and how you live.

When I see a deed of kindness, I am eager to be kind.
When a weaker brother stumbles and a strong man stays behind
Just to see if he can help him, then the wish grows strong in me
To become as big and thoughtful as I know that friend to be.
And all travelers can witness that the best of guides today
Is not the one who tells them, but the one who shows the way.

One good man teaches many, men believe what they behold;
One deed of kindness noticed is worth forty that are told.
Who stands with men of honor learns to hold his honor dear,
For right living speaks a language which to everyone is clear.
Though an able speaker charms me with his eloquence, I say,
I'd rather see a sermon than to hear one, any day.

While children may not always seem to listen to a parent's instructions, they will certainly watch a parent's actions. We must act and live in agreement with our words. Be a man or woman who follows Jesus. This applies to all the authority figures in your child's life. Be careful who you allow to be your child's role model. Parents must:

- Monitor their media choices. Who are the actors, YouTubers, TikTokers, Instagramers, and social celebrities that capture

162

your child's attention? Which social media platforms are prominent on their electronic devices? Are they viewing programs where extramarital sex is commonplace?

- Guide their reading selections. Have you read the books that are on the school's summer reading list? Do you buy books that have any inclination toward sorcery, magic, vampires, and demonic themes? What about "harmless" romance novels?
- Screen their music preferences. Are the performers and performances appropriate? Have you really listened to the words? What kind of suggestive behavior will children view on music videos?
- Scrutinize their sports heroes. Do the players exemplify good moral behavior on and off the field or court?

I think parents must invest the time into researching the backgrounds, characteristics, attitudes, agendas, politics, and motivations of anyone who is an influence on their children. It is not easy. It is time-consuming and tedious. Your children may not like it; in fact, they may get angry and defensive. Do it anyway.

Parents have not always been diligent in controlling the things that cry for children's attention. I know that many Christian parents have failed to take the necessary steps of teaching and training their children in godliness. We have failed to be active in keeping our children from harmful influences. Perhaps we have simply trusted them to discern on their own. Perhaps we have been too busy. Perhaps we did not want to upset them by getting into their personal business. Perhaps this is why we don't blush anymore.

If you like music, I suggest you listen to two relevant songs that touch on this issue. One is by Steve Green. "Guard Your Heart" from his album, *The Mission*, reminds us that we must be attentive to what grabs our attention. It only takes a moment of temptation to lure our children from the right path. When that happens, tragic consequences can occur.

The other song is "Slow Fade," sung by Casting Crowns on their album, *The Altar and the Door*. This song speaks to the truth that evil sometimes creeps into our lives over time. When we allow one small turn from the right way, it is easier and easier to continue on the path to destruction. Then, we can no longer recognize right from wrong. We must live with the consequences of our choices.

God has instructed parents to guide children and be involved in their lives. We train by example (Lois and Eunice, 2 Timothy 1:5). We teach with our words. Fathers, in Ephesians 6:4b, bear the greater charge to teach and train their children. You may ask, "What if there is no father in the home?" Try asking a Godly male friend, trusted grandparents, or other family members to help teach and train your sons and daughters. I recommend going to your pastor and asking him to pray for you, as well as to suggest some mature and godly believers to assist in this most important task of rearing children.

In verse 6, "…in the way…" is very important. The "way" should be defined according to biblical standards. The "way" should be God's way. Specifically, Jesus said, "I am the way, and the truth, and the life" (John 14:6). In the book of Acts, believers were referred to by "the Way" more often than being called Christian. In addition, "… he should go…" underscores that all children are special, unique and created by a loving Heavenly Father. The instruction and dis-cipline that works for one child in a family may not work for the other children in that family. That specific directive calls parents to observe their children and discover the best way to teach and train according to the bent of the child. Numerous books are available on reaching children who have different personalities, character-istics, gifts, temperaments, developmental, and physical features.

There are plenty of helpful books on the market for teaching children valuable character traits or giving tips for child discipline and correction.

This book is not intended as a how-to manual for rearing children. And yet, several areas of family and community life contribute to the increase or decrease in civility and morality. The world is a cruel place and temptations abound. Our society is much different than 30, 40, or 50 years ago. Though it has always been the nature of some children, young or grown, to stray from positive childhood influences, the pull of self, the world, and evil are getting stronger. Many parents fail to hold the ropes and rear well-mannered children. Most importantly, we must make it our ambition to teach and train our children to follow Jesus, so they will be equipped to teach their own children and reach the world with the Good News of Jesus Christ.

The observation of Proverbs 22:6 is that children brought up in a Christian home, under the influence of godly parents, will follow that teaching throughout their lives. Deuteronomy 6:4-9 provides a comprehensive overview of family life:

1. Believe God, 6:4
2. Love God, 6:5
3. Know and obey God's commandments, 6:6
4. Parents, especially fathers, teach the commandments to your children, 6:7
5. Parents, especially fathers, infuse the commandments into your doing and your thinking, 6:8
6. Mark your house as a believer's house, 6:9

Think about the following key areas of home and community life:

## Sharing

Let us begin with the truth statement that God owns it all; everything that we have is from Him. We are trustees, or managers, of it all. We are called to steward our relationships, our resources (I Chronicles 29:10-14), and our time (Ephesians 5:15; Psalm 90). What He has provided for us, He desires that we gladly share with others.

Children have to be taught to share. That may seem like a "duh" statement, but we all struggle with selfishness and greed, wanting our own way and all the goodies we can collect. By sharing, I am not simply referring to sharing possessions or toys, although it begins here when children are at their most impressionable. Parents don't always practice the discipline of sharing in front of their children. We aren't always intentional about discussing the action of sharing, much less the scriptural guidelines for sharing with others.

Do our children, grandchildren, nieces, and nephews see us give joyfully at church? Have we taught our kids to give regularly to the financial support of our church? "…for God loves a cheerful giver" (2 Corinthians 9:7). We read in Hebrews, "Do not neglect to do good and to share what you have, for such sacrifices are pleasing to God" (Hebrews 13:16).

How often do we share in the troubles of someone else? The Philippian church was praised by Paul for sharing in his difficulties; they provided for his needs (Philippians 4:14-16). Likewise, Paul encourages believers to share in comforting others who experience trials and afflictions (2 Corinthians 1:3-7). Some church members who have walked "…through the valley of the shadow of death" (Psalm 23:4) participate in support groups such as GriefShare.

What evangelism course have we enrolled in, or enrolled our children in, so that we can share the Gospel? "… and I pray that the sharing of your faith may become effective for the full knowledge of every good thing that is in us for the sake of Christ" (Philemon 1:6).

Here is a tough one. How are we to respond when we are crit-icized or persecuted for our faith? We should not be ashamed to suffer as a Christian. Peter tells Christ-followers to not be surprised at the struggles we experience in life, "…But rejoice insofar as you share Christ's sufferings… Yet if anyone suffers as a Christian, let him not be ashamed, but let him glorify God in that name" (1 Peter 4:12-16). Paul adds, "that I may know him and the power of his resurrection, and may share his sufferings, becoming like him in his death, that by any means possible I may attain the resurrection from the dead" (Philippians 3:10-11).

How often have we taken our children to serve meals to the homeless or to share our clothing with the poor? Have your local policemen, firemen, medical personnel, or teachers been on the receiving end of a plate of cookies, a thank-you note, or a gift card of appreciation? Does your church participate in Samaritan's Purse shoeboxes? If not, why don't you and your kids start this ministry at your church? Do you speak English? Why not get involved in your local English as a Second Language ministry? This is a fan-tastic approach to sharing the Gospel with people from around the world.

There are many ways to practice sharing. Start early with your children. Then, when the child is older, he or she will have devel-oped the habit and the conviction that this is a way to honor the Lord. Americans have been richly blessed; let us give in accord with what we have been given.

## Language

"Therefore, having put away falsehood, let each one of you speak the truth with his neighbor, for we are members one of another … Let no corrupting talk come out of your mouths, but only such as is good for building up, as fits the occasion, that it may give grace to those who hear" (Ephesians 4:25, 29). We need to teach our children to speak positive words into other people's lives. A little further we read, "Let there be no filthiness nor foolish talk nor crude joking, which are out of place, but instead let there be thanksgiving" (Ephesians 5:4).

Just from those few verses we ought to be ashamed of the language in our homes, among our friends and family, and in our communities. Why don't more of us blush about this problem? Is this an important subject? Is there an issue with language in our Christian homes? Absolutely, there is.

All around us is the irritating sound of clatter and dissonance. I have to admit that I regularly get embarrassed by the foul and disrespectful language I hear. We can't escape it. By language, I'm referring to the cursing, disrespect, arguing, lying, anger, slander, and bitterness that pour from our mouths daily. Whining, tattling, and sass are other areas of bad language.

It has become common-place to hear "Oh my god!" We hear it all the time on our TVs, on the radio, and from our friends. We hear it so often we don't even think about it. Do you say it? What about using "OMG" in your texting? Each one of us knows exactly what that "G" stands for. It's lame to say that you mean "gosh" instead of God's precious name. His name is, indeed, precious and holy, to be spoken reverently and in awe.

James 3 is a great chapter to read about a little part of our body that can do immense damage, to ourselves and to others. We cannot tame our tongue, but God can.

> It is a restless evil, full of deadly poison. With it we bless our Lord and Father, and with it we curse people who are made in the likeness of God. From the same mouth come blessing and cursing. My brothers, these things ought not to be so. Does a spring pour forth from the same opening both

fresh and salt water? Can a fig tree, my brothers, bear olives, or a grapevine produce figs? Neither can a saltpond yield fresh water. (James 3:8-12)

I encourage all of us to consider how often we speak graciously to someone at Walmart and then get in our car and flay them up one side and down another — in front of little listening ears. Church members have been known to compliment the preacher on his sermon as they exit the church, and then criticize him at the dinner table–again, in front of their children.

As a parent, grandparent, uncle, teacher, coach, or friend, all must model positive verbal communications to our children. There can be no debate. Don't use bad language and teach children that it is unacceptable, no matter what others say. As parent and protector of your children, you should hold all of your child's leaders to account for their speech. Insist on a curse-free environment. As a coach or teacher, be aware that you are a model for your players and students. Keep your speech in check.

Our language and our tempers go hand-in-hand. Anger often leads to foul and abusive language. James writes, "Know this, my beloved brothers: let every person be quick to hear, slow to speak, slow to anger; for the anger of man does not produce the righteousness of God. Therefore put away all filthiness and rampant wickedness." (James 1:19-21)

## Temper

Children are watching you. If parents display an uncontrolled temper, it will be etched in children's minds as a normal part of family life. "Fathers, do not provoke your children to anger..." (Ephesians 6:4a). This can be a generational pattern with deep, abiding scars.

Admittedly, controlling the temper tantrums of a child can be difficult at times. However, most temper issues can be avoided if children are trained early how to behave. It will take love – affectionate, uplifting, consistent, and intentional love. It will also take discipline, carried out tenderly, but with absoluteness. Parents must learn to be the firm authority in their child's life.

Parents must choose to expect certain proper actions from their children as they train them in civility and good manners.

Helping and teaching children to control the temper will provide the necessary habits for use in adulthood to overcome the inevitable conflict with abusive people and stressful situations with others that we all face.

The writer of Proverbs 15:18 clearly explains that someone who is quickly angered, someone who loses control of their emotions, creates anger among others. He or she causes the situation to escalate. It gets out of control. However, the writer goes on to say, someone who has self-control calms down the situation and has the wisdom to think before acting rashly. The above Proverb says, "A hot-tempered man stirs up strife, but he who is slow to anger quiets contention."

## Self-Control

When God introduces Himself to Moses at Mt. Sinai, one of the characteristics he attributes to Himself is self-control. He is the God who is slow to anger. This description is so significant that it is echoed multiple times throughout the Old Testament. (Numbers 14:18; Nehemiah 9:17; Psalm 86:15; Psalm 103.8; Psalm 145:8; Joel 2:13; Jonah 4:2; and Nahum 1:3)

In the book of Proverbs, the self-controlled man is patient and slow to anger. Solomon writes that "A man without self-control is like a city broken into and left without walls" (Proverbs 25:28). This man or woman has no defense against the enemy. He or she has no boundaries for right and wrong; anything is acceptable and the bad mixes with the good. In Titus 1, overseers were required to have the attribute of being slow to anger. James says that followers of Christ are to be characterized by patience and slowness to anger. This characteristic begins with God and should be reflected in the character of believers.

So what does being slow to anger have to do with self-control? The two areas in which men and women, boys and girls seem to have little control is with our tongue and with our temper. James couples them together, slow to speak and slow to wrath. When we are slow to wrath, we are reflecting God's character. "The LORD passed before him and proclaimed, 'The LORD, the LORD, a God merciful and gracious, slow to anger, and abounding in steadfast love and faithfulness...'" (Exodus 34:6)

It is a beautiful thing to see young and old display patience in the midst of trying circumstances. Daily, we face rude and cantankerous people. Children with no parental restraint, have selfish and greedy tendencies which usually deteriorate into loss of control of their emotions and actions. Parents, again, must model self-control. Parents must practice self-control so that arguing, tirades, and bickering are not habitual in the home. Parental action is the master teacher.

As we have seen throughout this book, we don't blush anymore. We, Americans in particular, but to a larger degree, all people, have forgotten, or chosen, to live freely and without restraint in civil and moral behaviors.

Self-control is one of the fruits of the spirit – a characteristic of God, borne out by the working of the Holy Spirit, to desire and to do the will of God. It is combined with love, joy, peace, patience, kindness, goodness, faithfulness, and gentleness. All of these are necessary for followers of Jesus. What a great world we would live in if we all practiced these actions. We would have no need to blush.

Yet, because of our disobedient nature and lack of self-control, our homes, nation, and world suffer.

Martin Luther King, Jr., demonstrating self-control over the injustices done to the black race, chose to advocate peaceful protests and share with the world that he looked forward to the day when character, rather than color, directed respectful interaction: "…I have a dream…that my children…will be judged by the content of their character…"

## Respect

When we have regard for the feelings, rights, or traditions of others, we are giving respect. Respect is due in many areas of life. This is, again, a parent's duty to demonstrate respect themselves, as well as teaching and training their children to give respect.

In our world of disrespect for God, man, and country, a family will go against the flow by practicing consideration for others. As Dave Ramsey says, "Live like no one else, so later you can Live Like No One Else." To put it another way, "Do not be conformed to this world, but be transformed by the renewal of your mind…" (Romans 12:2). When we act right, think right, believe right, speak right, we are living in a way that is both unique and extraordinary. Let us not assume that we merit salvation through right behavior and the attitude of respect. We will see in Chapter 16 that it is only through receiving God's free gift of salvation through faith in Jesus Christ that we are saved from eternal separation from God. Let us agree that many people do not give respect to anyone or anything in our country today. But, you will be "like No One Else" when you:

Respect God.
Respect human life, which bears His Image.
Respect your parents.
Respect your elders.

Respect our authorities.
Respect the flag.
Respect our military.
Respect people of other cultures.
Respect law enforcement officers.

In Romans 13, followers of Christ are instructed to respect those in authority – the teacher, preacher, principal, law enforcement officers, elders, and so on; Romans 14 guides the believer to respect the personal convictions of fellow believers. If a child does not learn to respect the authority of parents, it is very likely that he or she will never respect any authority. The foundation for children is Ephesians 6:1-3: "Children, obey your parents in the Lord, for this is right. 'Honor your father and mother' (this is the first commandment with a promise), 'that it may go well with you and that you may live long in the land.'"

## Divorce

The topic of divorce can be very painful for many people. This action destroys families, hopes, dreams, livelihoods, and futures. An article by Southern Methodist University's online newspaper reports that in 2020 approximately 39% of all marriages in America ended in divorce. While this percentage is down from previous years, it is still a sad fact that love and commitment seem to have faded away and convenience has taken priority. Recent studies show that millennials are choosing to wait longer to get married, or don't get married at all. They tend to live together first before deciding to tie the knot.

It is interesting to discover the divorce rate by profession. You will find different percentages at different internet sites, but "Occupations with the highest, and lowest divorce rate" from *Men of Valour* reports that the jobs with the highest divorce rates in the United States are:

- dancers and choreographers 43%
- bartenders 38%
- massage therapists 38%
- gaming cage workers and extruding machine operators 35%
- gaming service workers 31%

Professions with the lowest chances for divorce are:

- Farmers 8%
- Podiatrists 7%
- Clergy 6%
- Optometrists 4%
- Agricultural Engineers 2 %

So, you who are looking for a good life-long mate, go find an Agricultural Engineer and enjoy life.

We are fully aware that domestic violence, drug abuse, abandonment, and infidelity are strong factors for divorce. So, it is with caution that we speak of divorce as being convenient. No matter the reason for a disillusion of a covenant between two people, lives are affected long-term.

One of the key reasons for America's divorce rate is addressed in 2 Corinthians 6:14-18. Review the earlier part of this chapter; along with supervising your child's music and social media, you must be zealous to oversee your children's friends, especially when they begin to date. Christian parents must impress upon their children, while they are still in the home, not to be yoked with unbelievers. This does not mean that Christians are to exclude themselves from unbelievers, else how would the lost find Jesus? In the areas of dating, marriage, and business is where we apply this principle. The term "yoked" in verse 14 was in the immediate context of entering into a business partnership with someone who was not a Christ-follower. The broader implication has been understood by Christians to warn against marriage between believers and unbelievers. Since Christians and non-Christians operate from separate worldviews (or to use computer terminology — different operating systems), Paul is instructing believers to avoid entering into binding, long-term covenant relationships with unbelievers. This is in keeping with his previous letter in which he instructs believers to adjudicate among themselves rather than to sue one another and take each other to court among unbelievers. (1 Corinthians 6:1-11)

I believe parents bear the responsibility for guarding their children from unequal partnerships. Young Christian people who date unbelievers do so at their own risk. Extreme care must be exercised by parents to divert the influences of unbelievers who would lead their children away from the Lord. Love or lust sometimes blinds a young person's sense of obedience to biblical teachings. Help your child avoid heartache later in life by checking the faith and character of dating partners.

A somewhat popular alternative to dating is the practice of courting. Most people might think of this practice as common to the Duggar family, the Amish community, or early American settlers. The idea for this is solid. A young man and young woman get to know one another in the presence of family members. With no opportunity to be alone and sexually tempted, focus is on their relationship, their beliefs, expectations, dreams, and character. Courting is not a preference for all relationships. However, when two people invest time in getting to know one another without the pressure of sexual activity, commitments are often well thought out. Evidence of dysfunctional tendencies can be rooted out before marriage, and assurance of comparable Christian beliefs are satisfied.

Sometimes it appears that all the training invested into a child's life has been in vain. The child, or young adult, has strayed far from the pathway of righteousness. The parent feels like a failure. He or she may go to the grave with the weight of that burden. But, if parents have been obedient to the Lord, if they have been faithful to witnessing to their children and setting a Christian example, then they should trust God with the results. Leave the burden of remorse and failure in His hands. It is also possible that as the child approaches his or her end of days, the Christian teaching of childhood may rise up within the heart and a miracle would happen for the saving of their soul before they go to meet the Lord. The key to all of this is the parents' responsibility to bring their child(ren) up in the discipline and instruction of the Lord. If that is done faithfully, parental obligations have been met and future decisions lie in the heart of the children. Read Ezekiel 18.

We started this chapter with the negative effects of absentee dads on the lives of children. Where are the dads who will protect and provide for their children? Where are the dads who will model their Heavenly Father to their children? Which dads will lead their children to Jesus? We need men in this country who will commit to godly fatherhood. I am convinced that men are needed to lead their families. Single moms deserve praise and thanks for all that they do. They need support for their heavy load.

The positive statistics from the *National Fatherhood Initiative* reveal that children with involved dads:

- have better emotional and social well-being
- are less likely to be mistreated
- do better in school
- are less likely to carry guns and deal drugs

- have fewer behavior and fewer psychological problems
- have a higher likelihood of getting mostly A's in school
- are less likely to engage in risky sexual behavior
- have less stress

Closing out this chapter, we are reminded of a 2011 movie about fatherhood entitled *Courageous: Honor Begins at Home*. The Kendrick Brothers, supported by Sherwood Baptist Church in Albany, Georgia, share a powerful story that will convict and inspire hearts toward home and family. I highly recommend that you watch it.

# Chapter Sixteen

# TURNING IT AROUND

*"If my people, which are called by my name, shall humble themselves, and pray, and seek my face, and turn from their wicked ways, then will I hear from heaven, and will forgive their sin, and will heal their land."*

2 Chronicles 7:14 KJV

*"That if thou shalt confess with thy mouth the Lord Jesus, and shalt believe in thine heart that God hath raised him from the dead, thou shalt be saved. For with the heart man believeth unto righteousness; and with the mouth confession is made unto salvation."*

Romans 10:9-10 KJV

This book is intended to bring to your attention the lack of civility in today's society. Bad manners, rudeness, insolence, and vulgarity are not life and death matters; however, they ought to be matters of shame and embarrassment when we view these actions as a transgression of a standard of polite behavior. We don't blush anymore, and we should.

Through this book I hope to encourage a dad or mom to pause and contemplate their interactions with their children, and to pursue a kinder, and more loving dialogue. I want politicians to evaluate their oratory and present a more truthful and honest discourse. I pray that the hearts of people will be turned to think about the words of their mouths and the actions of their hearts so they will be more in tune with biblical teachings.

The idea of "Turning It Around" is a call to turn from self-ishness, pride, and bad behavior to gentleness, respect, gracious behavior, and a higher mindset of living in relationship with others. Most importantly, it is a call to repentance and faith in Jesus Christ.

Probably one of the most difficult tasks in life is to stop the pro-verbial boulder from rolling downhill. The boulder has no concern for anyone in the way. That is the scenario facing society today as we see the declining of morals, character, civility, and values. That rush has swept across our nation with amazing speed, destroying anyone in its path. Concerned citizens who stand for righteousness and truth are often crushed, shamed, and belittled for proclaiming a better way of life. It will take more than a single pocket of resis-tance. It will take all of us, from the youngest to the oldest, through all walks of life, in every part of this great land to turn it around.

Our good friend, Paul, writes:

> That in the last days there will come times of dif-ficulty. For people will be lovers of self, lovers of money, proud, arrogant, abusive, disobedient to their parents, ungrateful, unholy, heartless, unap-peasable, slanderous, without self-control, brutal, not loving good, treacherous, reckless, swollen with conceit, lovers of pleasure rather than lovers of God, having the appearance of godliness, but denying its power. Avoid such people. (2 Timothy 3:1-5)

We see this in our society today.

Let's make sure of an important point here. The lack of good manners, politeness, civility, and blushing does not mean that a person is unsaved and bound for Hell. Conversely, in no way am I asserting that those with good manners and morals are assured of a place in Heaven. There is only one way to Heaven, and that is through faith in Christ Jesus. Jesus says, "I am the way, and the truth, and the life. No one comes to the Father except through me" (John 14:6-7). When we read Paul's description of the last days, we recognize these characteristics are prevalent all around us. The bigger issue is whether we are practicing these behaviors and attitudes. If we are, there is a need to turn around before it is too late.

Our opening Scripture for this chapter (2 Chronicles 7:14) summarizes a process when followers of God turn from their wickedness and turn back to Him for forgiveness and restoration of the relationship. Turning it around for God's errant children is initiated by the working of the Holy Spirit in your mind and heart. If we profess to be Christian, we ought to examine ourselves for right behavior. Are we living lives of holiness? Are we demonstrating behavior that leads people to Jesus? Are we seeking Jesus every day? Often we need to ask ourselves these questions.

What about those who are not God's children? Those who do not know God. How can they turn and be saved? The second opening Scripture (Romans 10:9-10) answers that question, and it is critical if lasting change is to be achieved individually, in our nation, and around the world.

For me, that turn around occurred when I was thirteen years old. I would like to say the trumpets of God sounded, the bells of heaven peeled forth, and the angels of God surrounded me with singing. But, in fact, nothing earth-shaking happened except my daddy gently touched me on my shoulder and asked, "Don't you think it's time?" Being brought up in one of the biggest churches in Akron, Ohio (The Akron Baptist Temple), and listening to Dallas F. Billington preach multiple sermons on accepting Jesus as Savior, I knew as soon as Daddy asked me that it was time to give my life to Jesus. I did just that. However, it didn't happen there at the big church. It happened in an old, one-room country church which was appropriately named the Country Baptist Church. We moved there to support a young and upcoming preacher–Billy Bradford. There, I was saved, but since we did not have a baptistry at the Country Church, I was baptized back at the Akron Baptist Temple by Billy, while my sweet daddy looked on with joy in his heart. The young prodigal had come home, and my earthly father rejoiced, as did my Heavenly Father.

It might be appropriate here to elaborate on my condition at the time of salvation. As a thirteen-year- old, I was a pretty good kid. I didn't smoke, drink, do drugs, engage in sexual activities, run with gangs, or commit gigantic sins. But I knew I was sinful and that the sin needed to be forgiven. That was only possible through the grace of the Lord Jesus. Have I sinned since that time? Absolutely, but praise be to God, He has promised that "If we confess our sins, he is faithful and just to forgive us our sins and to cleanse us from all unrighteousness" (1 John 1:9). We live in a world controlled by Satan who tempts us daily. Being human, we fall, and fail the commandment, "You shall be holy, for I am holy" (1 Peter 1:16). Through repentant prayer we are restored to righteousness (James 5:16).

The most important turn for every person, according to God's Holy Word, is to turn from a sinful life and accept Jesus as Lord and Savior. Here is how you can do that:

- "For I am not ashamed of the gospel, for it is the power of God for salvation to everyone who believes, to the Jew first and also to the Greek." (Romans 1:16)

I give my testimony of God's grace and His plan for salvation through the gospel, with the hope that you, too, will surrender yourself to the Lordship of Jesus Christ. Jesus said that there is no other way to the Father except through him. (John 14:6)

This book has been about our inability to blush. In our current social climate, having a confident faith in Jesus as the only Savior seems to require an apology. I am not ashamed to trust Jesus, and I pray that you will not be either. As you read the following verses and explanations, trust these words and share them with others.

- "...Let God be true though every one were a liar..." (Romans 3:4)

First, we must understand that God is Holy and true. We are not. Throughout Scripture, God reveals Himself as good, holy, righteous, perfect, and pure. Jesus states, "...No one is good except God alone" (Luke 18:19; Mark 10:18). God is our standard. Compared to His perfection, no one measures up. In contrast to His truth and trustworthiness, every human being is a liar. We do not tell the truth 100 percent of the time. We may lie by omission, we may tell fibs, we may stretch the truth, we may make false accusations, we may tell bold-faced lies, or we may commit perjury. God is true, and we are all liars. Unfortunately, we don't measure up to God's standard on any of the Commandments (see Ex. 20; Deut. 5).

- "...None is righteous, no, not one." (Romans 3:10)

While Romans 3:4 focuses on who God is, Romans 3:10 focuses on who we are. Since God is the standard of righteousness we can never come close to His perfection. In fact, the prophet Isaiah wrote, "We have all become like one who is unclean, and all our righteous deeds are like a polluted garment..." (Isaiah 64:6a).

Many times when we attend a funeral, the officiator refers to the deceased as a good person; they have entered Heaven because they were good. The fact is, good people do not go to Heaven, only saved people do. The Psalmist writes: "They have all turned aside; together they have become corrupt; there is none who does good, not even one" (Psalm 14:3).

Since God is the only One who is good, how can we ever get good enough to be with Him in Heaven?

- "for all have sinned and fall short of the glory of God." (Romans 3:23)

All people have sinned — disobeyed God's rules. The problem is, our moral and practical failings are not simply a thing of the past. For "all have sinned" – past tense, and we "fall short" – present tense; therefore, we continue to struggle with disobeying God. The Apostle Paul puts it this way in Romans 7:15-18, "...For I do not do what I want, but I do the very thing I hate ...For I know that nothing good dwells in me, ...For I have the desire to do what is right, but not the ability to carry it out ...but sin that dwells within me." Sin is our ongoing problem.

- "For the wages of sin is death..." (Romans 6:23a)

We earn death for our sin. What happens when we die? We all face a judgment (Hebrews 9:27). The verdict for our guilt is to be in a horrible place that God prepared for sinners to be punished forever – Hell. Not only will we face physical death, but we will face eternal separation from God forever. That's bad news.

- "but God shows his love for us in that while we were still sinners, Christ died for us." (Romans 5:8)

God showed His love for us by sending Jesus to die in our place (Romans 5:8). Ultimately, all sin, all disobedience to God, requires a death sentence (see Gen. 2:17; James 1:15). Someone must face the wrath of God for your sin. God has provided an antidote for the poison of sin. On the cross, Jesus not only faced physical pain and death, but He also took on the guilt of each one of us. He became the sin-bearer, and because of that, He took on God's wrath for sin. This is what Paul meant when he wrote, "...while we were still sinners..."

People try to do good things so that God will accept them into Heaven, such as going to church, helping others, or being nice, kind, and polite. These acts are not good enough for God. They will not take away our sin. We cannot do enough good works to please God's standard of perfection (Ephesians 2:9). But, JESUS did! "For God so loved the world [that's you and me], that he gave his only Son [Jesus], that whoever believes in him should not perish but have eternal life. For God did not send his Son into the world to condemn the world, but in order that the world might be saved through him. Whoever believes in him is not condemned, but whoever does not believe is condemned already, because he has not believed in the name of the only Son of God" (John 3:16-18).

- "...but the free gift of God is eternal life in Christ Jesus our Lord." (Romans 6:23b)

God's free gift to us is eternal life with Jesus. In the first part of this verse, we are told what we earn for remaining as unbelievers — death. This is what we earn, and what we face, when we refuse to surrender to Jesus as Master, as King, and as Substitute. This second half of the verse focuses on the gift God offers. It is something that cannot be earned, but something that must be received. Think of it as a Christmas present or birthday gift. Jesus is the

Christmas gift from God, and He marks your spiritual new birth. You have to receive Him. You have to open up the package. The gift inside is eternal life. This is good news!

- "Behold, I stand at the door and knock. If anyone hears my voice and opens the door, I will come in to him and eat with him, and he with me." (Revelation 3:20)

He is waiting for you to invite Him to be Lord and Savior of your life. Open the door to Him today.

- "because, if you confess with your mouth that Jesus is Lord and believe in your heart that God raised Him from the dead, you will be saved." (Romans 10:9-10)

Jesus did not remain in a tomb. God raised Him from the dead in fulfillment of His promise (see Psalm 16:10). This was a demonstration that God had accepted Jesus' sacrifice for all who would believe.

How can you receive the gift of God? These verses explain. You must become a disciple of Jesus. You must confess Him, not only as your sin-bearer, but as your King. You must believe that what He said about Himself is true. And you must obey what He says to you.

- "How then will they call on him in whom they have not believed? And how are they to believe in him of whom they have never heard? And how are they to hear without someone preaching? And how are they to preach unless they are sent? As it is written, 'How beautiful are the feet of those who preach the good news!'" (Romans 10:13-14)

Here is where the Gospel, the Good News, becomes personal. Those who are called to faith in Jesus are called to be both disciples and disciple-makers. We are invited to believe, and we are invited to tell others to believe. While this may seem like a frightening prospect, we are reminded to not be ashamed of telling about Jesus. Just as I am not ashamed to tell you, as you believe, you should not be ashamed to tell others. "So faith comes from hearing, and hearing through the word of Christ" (Romans 10:17).

If you have never turned to God, in the name of Jesus, this is the greatest turn-around you could do. Turn from your sin, turn to Jesus in faith that He died on the cross for your sin, that He was buried and raised to life after three days, and give Him control of your life. You will have a new life: "Therefore, if anyone is in Christ, he is a new creation. The old has passed away; behold, the new has come" (2 Corinthians 5:17).

Based on the selected issues addressed in this book, it is my hope that we have recognized the problems, and perhaps, wrestled with the ideas a little bit. During the writing process, my mind was on alert for the words shame, incivility, and blushing. It seemed I heard or saw those words everywhere. Many radio commentators voiced their opinions on the downward shift in morality that is evident in our country; people on social media were commenting about the need to love our country, respect our flag, obey the law, and practice good manners. Just recently, I came across this Facebook post:

Things money can't buy:

1. Manners
2. Morals
3. Respect
4. Character

5. Common Sense
6. Trust
7. Patience
8. Class
9. Integrity
10. Love

It's true; money cannot buy these attributes, but some, if not all, can be acquired with a turn to the One who is the standard-bearer of all of these beautiful characteristics. He gives the gift that is worth giving, the gift that is worth possessing, and the gift that lasts for eternity. I pray that as you read and ponder the thoughts I presented in this book and you will be awakened. May your heart be changed for the better, and may we each set an example of holy living as we strive to be more like Jesus Christ, the Son of God.

As I close out this chapter and this book, it is my hope and prayer that I have clearly stated the problems that we face about selfishness, pride, rudeness, and incivility, and what to do about them. My prayer is a return to gentleness, politeness, respect, sweet relationships with others, and love that knows no boundaries.

Go, dear friends, proclaim the loving kindness of the Lord, and share His goodness with family, friends, and foe alike. To God be the glory.

# FINAL THOUGHTS

As this book is being written, there is chaos in many streets across America. There are divisions within the congress of the United States, in homes, and in society more severe than at any time in our history except the Civil War. There are Democrats against Republicans, blacks against whites, liberals against conservatives, non-Christians against Christians, family members against family members and there is only One intercessor who can bring these groups together in unity. He is the Lord Jesus Christ.

Incivility runs deep in America. Rudeness and impoliteness reign throughout this country with no end in sight.

The observations and suggestions in this book may not be a panacea for all the ills facing the nation and its people, but they can be a starting place as a reminder that we have lost something very valuable in our everyday lives-respect and good manners toward one another. Many of the recommendations contained herein could be used to help us return to a people who, once again, show forth grace and love to all mankind.

Because of my age, I may not see any significant changes in society unless God performs an immediate miracle of enlightenment on the public. Maybe, just maybe, my grandchildren and great-grandchildren will be able to see and live in a more tranquil and benevolent world.

America has forgotten how to blush, and without that personal characteristic etched in human hearts and applied to everyday actions, the nation will not get any better. As a Christian, I believe in the eminent return of Jesus Christ to call His followers to eternal existence with Him in Heaven. I believe His return is soon. My hope is that, with the time that we have left, some hearts will be changed so that this country and world are better places in which to live.

May the peace of God reign in the hearts of all who have walked with me through the pages of this book. It has been a long time coming to finally see it in print. I have done my best to bring to your attention the status of our nation. As I have talked with friends and family members about the content of this book, each person has expressed frustration with the country as it is at present. So many of us fondly remember the past and wish for a better today.

May we all be better men and women, boys and girls, and rise to the level God created us to attain.

I have done my best, and I rest my case. God bless one and all.

RKP

# BIOGRAPHY
Robert Kenneth Parsons, Sr.

Robert was born in Akron, Ohio on June 11, 1931. He is the youngest of four children. He has been married to his wife, Maidee, for 67 years. They have two children, Robert Kenneth, Jr., and Kimberly P. Wilson. They have nine grandchildren and five great-grandchildren.

Robert served in the U.S. Air Force for four years during the time of the Korean War and he was discharged honorably in 1954.

After his military service, Robert received higher education at the University of Florida and graduated in 1958 with a Bachelor's Degree in Chemical Engineering. He then became a senior launch supervisor with Chrysler Corporation's Space Division at Cape Canaveral, Florida, in charge of design and operation of liquid hydrogen facilities. He participated in getting men on the moon in 1969. During this time, he also served as deacon and lay minister of music at First Baptist Church of Titusville, Florida.

In 1973, Robert and Maidee moved to Franklin, North Carolina, where Robert worked as Vice-President in a company that mined and processed wet ground mica. He also became a self-trained Pomologist and operated a 50-acre apple orchard. During the next twenty-five years, Robert served as deacon, music director, and Sunday School teacher in various churches.

Upon retirement in 1994, he and Maidee moved back to Florida and joined McGregor Baptist Church in Ft. Myers, Florida. There he was active as deacon, Sunday School teacher, Chairman of the local chapter of Child Evangelism Fellowship, and Director of the Men's Ministry at McGregor. The Men's Ministry grew to 250 men with 12 Bible study groups throughout the city. Robert prepared Bible study lessons for all these groups.

In 2006, Robert and Maidee moved to Ocala, Florida, where they became active members of College Road Baptist Church. He continues to serve as deacon, teacher, and Child Evangelism Fellowship teacher in the Good News Clubs, teaching Bible lessons to children in elementary school.

The Parsons are avid RVers. They have traveled more than 150,000 miles, visiting all contiguous states, Alaska, Canada, Mexico, Newfoundland, Nova Scotia, and all parts in-between.

At nearly 90 years of age, the desire to prepare Bible studies and teach God's Word is still the highest priority in Robert's life. He hopes to continue to serve the Lord until he is called Home.

# BIBLIOGRAPHY

"90 state lawmakers accused of sexual misconduct since 2017." *AP News*. The Associated Press. 2 Feb. 2019. Web. 29 Sept. 2020.

"Abortion Fast Facts." *CNN.com*. A Warner Media Company, 29 June 2020. Web. 26 Sept. 2020.

Adler, Mortimer J., and Charles van Doren. *How to Read a Book*. New York: Simon & Schuster, 2014. Print.

Advocating Overthrow of Government 1940 ed. Title 18 U.S. Code Section 2385. *Legal Information Institute*. Cornell Law School. Web. 29 Nov. 2020.

"Anarchy." *Webster's New World College Dictionary*. 5th ed. 2020. Print.

"Black Lives Matter 13 Guiding Principles." *D.C. Area Educators for Social Justice*. A Project of Teaching for Change. n.d. Web. 4 Oct. 2020.

Brandenburg v. Ohio. 395 U. S. 444. Supreme Court of the US. 1969. *Justia Legal Resources*, n.d. Web. 29 Nov. 2020.

"Civil." *American Dictionary of the English Language*. 1st ed. 1828. Print.

"Civil." *Webster's New World College Dictionary*. 5th ed. 2020. Print.

Clark, James. "7 Humbling Excerpts From George Washington's Farewell Address As America's First President." *Task & Purpose.* Grid North Group, 17 Sept. 2015. Web. 13 Nov. 2020.

"Cleanliness is next to godliness." *Dictionary.com.* Houghton Mifflin Harcourt Publishing Company, n.d. Web. 29 Nov. 2020.

Collier, Jeremy. *A Short View of the Immorality, and Profaneness of the English Stage, Together With the Sense of Antiquity upon this Argument. Project Gutenberg.* Public Domain. Web. 9 Nov. 2020.

"Common sense." *Webster's New World College Dictionary.* 5th ed. 2020. Print.

"Conscience." *Webster's New World College Dictionary.* 5th ed. 2020. Print.

Daly, John. "John Daly: What Is Etiquette and Where Did It Originate?" *Noozhawk.* Malamute Ventures LLC, 12 Aug. 2014. Web. 11 Nov. 2020.

Denzel Washington. "With so many things..." *Instagram.* 17 Apr. 2019. instagram.com/p/BwXM3PnlzJo/?hl=en

DeSilver, Drew. "U.S. students' academic achievement still lags that of their peers in many other countries." *Pew Research Center.* The Pew Charitable Trusts. 15 Feb. 2017. Web. 27 Sept. 2020.

"Eclectic." *Webster's New World College Dictionary.* 5th ed. 2020. Print.

Engel v. Vitale. Supreme Court of the US. 1962. Bill of Rights Institute, n.d. Web. 11 Nov. 2020.

Erickson. *What would the world be like without The United States of America?* Mr. Erickson Rules! 13 Feb. 2020. Web. 29 Nov. 2020.

"Foundation." *Webster's New World College Dictionary*. 5th ed. 2020. Print.

Greer, Alex. "Some of the Biggest Congressional Scandals in History." *US & World News*. Business2Community. 19 Aug. 2015. Web. 30 Sept. 2020.

Guest, Edgar. "Sermons We See." *Your Daily Poem.com*. Your Daily Poem, n.d. N. pag. Web. 22 Oct. 2020.

"Henry Lee." *Encyclopaedia Britannica*. Encyclopaedia Britannica, Inc., 21 March 2020. Web. 29 Nov. 2020.

"How Frequently are People Divorcing in 2020?" *SMU Daily Campus*. Southern Methodist University. 21 Feb. 2020. Web. 23 Oct. 2020.

Jefferson, Thomas. Letter to the Danbury Baptist Association. 1802. *Letters Between Thomas Jefferson and the Danbury Baptists*. Bill of Rights Institute, n.d. Web. 9 Nov. 2020.

Konecny, Tom. "George Washington's Prayer at Valley Forge." *Meet America*. N.p. n.d. Web. 28 Sept. 2020.

Lee, MJ, Sunlen Serfaty, and Juana Summers. "Congress paid out $17 million in settlements.

Here's why we know so little about that money." *CNN Politics*. A Warner Media Company. 16 Nov. 2017. Web. 29 Sept. 2020.

"Legislator Misconduct Database." *govtrack*. Civic Impulse, LLC. n.d. Web. 29 Sept. 2020.

Litton, Ed. "Get Ready for the Coming Political Crisis: Lifestyles of a Christian Citizen." Redemption Church. Saraland, Alabama. 4 Oct. 2020. Sermon.

Livingston, Gretchen. "About one-third of U.S. children are living with an unmarried parent." *Pew Research Center*. The Pew Charitable Trusts. 27 Apr. 2018. Web. 24 Sept. 2020.

McClung, Floyd. *Living on the Devil's Doorstep*. Seattle: YWAM Publishing, 2001. Print.

McDonald III, John T. "The Death of Common Sense." *The Times Union*. The Hearst Corporation. 1 Oct. 2013. Web. 2 Oct. 2020.

McGuffey, William H. *McGuffey's Eclectic Readers*. Ed. Jean Morton. Milford, MI: Mott Media, Inc., 1982. Print.

McKinney, Michael D. "George Washington's Rules of Civility & Decent Behavior in Company and Conversation." *Foundations Magazine*. M2 Communications. n.d. Web. 5 Oct. 2020.

Miss Manners. *Facebook*. www.facebook.com/officialmissmanners/. Accessed 11 Nov. 2020.

Nadales, Gabriel. "Antifa is anti-America and its values." *The Hill*. Capitol Hill Publishing Corp., 6 Dec. 2019. Web. 29 Nov. 2020.

National Organization for Women. *National Organization for Women*. NOW, 2020. Web. 8 Nov. 2020.

Newport, Frank. "2017 Update on Americans and Religion." *Gallup*. N.p. 22 Dec. 2017. Web. 6 Oct. 2020.

"Occupations with the highest, and lowest rate divorce rate." *Men of Valour ...unleash the man in you*. The Men of Valour, n.d. Web. 14 Nov. 2020.

Olivastro, Andrew, and Mike Gonzalez. "Like the Soviets, Black Lives Matter Purges its History." *The Heritage Foundation*. 23 Sept. 2020. Web. 4 Oct. 2020.

Paine, Thomas. "The Crisis." *USHistory.org.* Independence Hall Association, n.d. Web. 8 Nov. 2020.

Rosenthal, Marv. "Defining the Church." *Zion's Fire* July-Aug. 2020: 10-13. Print.

Shaffer, Kent. "Fun-Filled Church Events: Are They Missing the Point?" *Preach It Teach It.* N.p. n.d. Web. 13 Oct. 2020.

Smith, Alan. "15 other presidents who were caught up in salacious sex scandals before Trump's Stormy Daniels saga." *Business Insider.* 9 Apr. 2018. Web. 29 Sept. 2020.

Smith, Kate. "Abortion at "historic low" by all measures, new CDC study says." *CBS News.* CBS Interactive, Inc., 27 Nov. 2019. Web. 26 Sept. 2020.

Steinbuch, Yaron. "Black Lives Matter co-founder describes herself as 'trained Marxist.'" *nypost.com.* New York Post, 25 June 2020. Web. 10 Nov. 2020.

The Charter of Massachusetts Bay. 1629. *The Avalon Project Documents in Law, History and Diplomacy.* Yale Law School, 2008. Web. 21 Sept. 2020.

*The Emily Post Institute.* The Emily Post Institute, Inc., n.d. Web. 11 Nov. 2020.

*The Holy Bible.* Wheaton: Crossway, 2001. Print. English Standard Version.

"The Maxims of Ptah-Hotep: Book & Instructions." *Study.com.* Working Scholars, 17 Oct. 2017. Web. 11 Nov. 2020.

*The New-England Primer.* 1777. Foreword David Barton. Aledo, TX: WallBuilder Press, 2009. Print.

"The New-England Primer." *Encyclopaedia Britannica.* Encyclopaedia Britannica, Inc., 4 March 2019. Web. 29 Nov. 2020.

"The Proof Is In: Father Absence Harms Children." *National Fatherhood Initiative.* N.p. n.d. Web. 24 Sept. 2020.

"Truth." *Webster's New World College Dictionary.* 5th ed. 2020. Print.

United States. Federal Courts. U.S. Judicial Branch. "Facts and Case Summary – Texas v. Johnson." *United States Courts.* Federal Judiciary, n.d. Web. 9 Nov. 2020.

Waggoner, Michael D. "When the Court Took on Prayer and the Bible in Public Schools." Rev. of *The Bible, the School, and the Constitution: The Clash That Shaped Modern Church-State Doctrine,* auth. Steven K. Green. *Religion & Politics: Fit for Polite Company.* Washington University in St. Louis, 25 June 2012. Web. 11 Nov. 2020.

Warren, Roland. "Black Lives Matter's Real Agenda." *washingtontimes.com.* The Washington Times, 28 July 2016. Web. 10 Nov. 2020.

Webster, Noah. *The Original Blue Back Speller.* 1824. San Antonio, TX: The Vision Forum, Inc., 2009. Print.

Westerhoff III, John H. *McGuffey and His Readers: Piety, Morality, and Education in Nineteenth-Century America.* Milford, MI: Mott Media, 1982. Print.

"Who are Antifa?" *ADL: Fighting Hate for Good.* Anti-Defamation League, n.d. Web. 11 Nov. 2020.

CPSIA information can be obtained
at www.ICGtesting.com
Printed in the USA
LVHW070125130521
687236LV00017B/600